Rash Acts

ALSO BY BISHOP & FULLER:

Wanna
Full Hookup
Smitty's News
Mine Alone
Dakota Bones
Okiboji
Disconnects
Dreambelly
Action News
Marie Antoinette
Le Cabaret de Camille (with Camilla Schade)
The Chimes (after Dickens)
Amazed (after Flaminio Scala)
Marvels (after Carlo Gozzi)
Medea / Sacrament (after Euripides)
Goners (after Matthew G. Lewis)

Conrad Bishop & Elizabeth Fuller

RASH ACTS

Eighteen Snapshots for the Stage

*an anthology of short dramatic work
from twenty years of touring repertory*

WordWorkers Press
Lancaster

RASH ACTS:
Eighteen Snapshots for the Stage

WordWorkers
www.independenteye.org
eye@independenteye.org

First printing November 1989
ISBN: 0-9624511-3-4
Library of Congress Catalog Card Number: 89-51731

Cover design by Mark Stoner

Contents

Thanks. . .

To the Theatre X and Independent Eye ensembles, to students at University of Delaware, to participants in workshops cross-country who worked in the creation of these pieces, and especially to Camilla Schade.

To Lloyd Richards, Jon Jory, Marshall Mason, John Schneider, Flora Coker, Barbara Schneider, Lucy Kroll — these special among many others — for encouraging an all-consuming addiction to writing for the stage.

To Leon Katz, Gerald Hiken, Ted Hoffman, Carl Weber, and Alvina Krause for academic training that's actually stood the test of time.

To Phil Arnoult, Carol Baish, Chris Hayes, Sharon Phillips, Dick Mennen and others for hosting our work before we had a home, and to Stephen Patterson, Duff May, Anne Gardner, John Synodinos and trustees of the Eye for giving us a home at last.

To Peter Carnahan, Jessica Andrews, Marcia Salvatore, Dick Aumiller, Tim Cooley and Dorothy Louise for support in a great many ways. To Eli and Johanna Bishop for patience, inspiration, and hard work. And to Margaret Leuck for lessons in survival.

RASH ACTS

Eighteen Snapshots for the Stage

PREFACE

From 1969 until 1988, we wrote dramatic acts —
several hundred total — for touring ensembles with
whom we performed. In 33 states, we encountered vir-
tually every audience, every occasion for theatre, and
what often felt like every church basement, black-box
theatre, prison rec room, college cafeteria, high school
gym and institutional multi-purpose room in America.
Not unlike Moliere's years in the provinces, except that
we never chanced to play before the King.

During these actor-manager years, we rarely had
occasion to think of ourselves as playwrights. We simply crafted words for our fellow actors and ourselves.
Some sketches began as improvisations; others were
written straight out. Often, writing combined the
skills of matchmaker and obstetrician: catching a faint
glint, mating it with a story from one place, characters
from another, a comic bit that was an actor's schtick-
of-last-resort but which might be charged with new
meaning. And then we assisted the birth. Often that
meant not writing it fully but only establishing the
units of action, setting just the cue lines that moved
the improvised segments to the next wave of the story.
Gradually, the writer began to intrude implacably,
with more focus to the precision of the words; and in
1980, when we started to write full-length plays for
other stages, our writing took new directions. These
sketches betray their origins as facilitators of a collec-
tive vision rather than as solo expressions. In some
ways, a weakness; in others, a strength.

The sketch form came to dominate our work, for a
time, by pure chance. Our first Theatre X revue in
1969 was a revue by default. Three months of experimental improvisation, at odd hours in odder locations
in the backwaters of Milwaukee, had re-invented all
the chief progressive impulses of the 1960's, but with
little coherent direction to the work. In desperation,
we scheduled a show six weeks thereafter, titled it,
found a space, designed a poster with a large hole cut
out of the center and a picture of a hot dog resting on a
bed of spikes: a metaphor for our utter lack of a notion
of what the show would be.

What evolved was a patchwork, compiled from the bright ideas, improvisations and plagiarisms of its 18-member cast. Its tattered brashness, mad stew of styles and gut humanity all contributed to the popularity of **X COMMUNICATION**; and it continued endless evolutions in tour repertory for the next five years. At this time, the traditions of vaudeville routine, Second City cabaret skit and Story Theatre fable were crossbreeding with new impulses from agitprop, Teatro Campesino's "actos," The Living Theatre's literalized ceremonials, Open Theatre's mythic transformations; and we, like countless other new groups of the time, piled our plates high from the smorgasbord.

For a fledgling company, the revue sketch had real benefits. A sketch could be added any time, and the stage could reflect the kaleidoscopic diversity of real life in concentrated, potent capsule form. Shows could be assembled for any occasion: coffee-house entertainment, high school assembly, church service, peace rally, arts fair or prison visit. This heady impulse to be all things to all people wasn't without risk. Hired by a rock promoter to provide a diverting interlude between acts of a "50's Rock Revival" concert, we found ourselves playing to 10,000 frenzied fans — not fans of ours — just after Chuck Berry, right before Little Richard. Most of the debris hurled at us didn't connect. Some did.

These sketches reflect that early diversity, but they have a common spine. For us, style has never been an end in itself, only a means to find the *appropriate language* for a story. Our focus is on behavior: what do people *do*? What they *feel* is coloration of the act, but a play is more than an emotional Jacuzzi or a framed image. One sort of revue sketch — e.g. countless TV interview parodies — involves setting up a comic premise, milking it for jokes, then getting out fast. Instead, we focus on what changes, or tries to change but doesn't, or seemed to change but didn't. The title of a popular Theatre X football skit (contributed by our friend, the wiener-on-spikes artist) might in fact apply to most of our acts: **Sculptured Meat in Motion**. Sometimes, amid frantic rush-hour scrambles, all that really moves is the minute hand; yet that stasis is charged with energy.

All this work has been performed for extremely diverse audiences, ranging from people who'd never seen theatre before to some who'd seen a lot more than they wanted to. Breadth of style has rarely been a problem: while we use the free play of presentational metaphor, all the acts are based in the *recognizable*. It can be more difficult for audiences — and for actors — to understand that an *ambivalent response* is actually desirable. We sometimes begin work on a piece with no notion whether it will be funny or grim or both. Its coloration is in complementary hues, not in a single flat wash. We are so accustomed to drama, films or music prescribing our response that it may be genuinely uncomfortable to feel that our hearts and our brains are actually our own. The actor must let the audience surprise themselves.

We aim for drama that's an *act* perpetrated in front of an audience, something as real as swiping a wallet or kissing the nearest spectator. We start with the concrete, then find its energy from what's at stake in it for *us*. The challenge is to create entertaining work from subject matter — human limits — which teeters on tastelessness. Some would prefer Reality with a remote switch: tune out what we're just not ready to face. But in fact, comedy is nothing if it's not about human limits, and that puts us all at risk. We're all that top-hatted dignitary walking down the sidewalk, chin aloft, thinking our wisdom, youth or age are insurance against the banana peel, death, divorce or Deuteronomy. The Oz Scarecrow, brainless and flammable, dances in an unquenchable quest; we can't join him unless we're willing to be surprised.

This summer we were reading classic farces and watching horror movies. Strange combination, but with many similarities. In horror flicks, our hero faces real death in all its most imaginative forms. In farce, nobody gets sliced into appetizers, but the threat is precisely the same. What's at stake is *symbolic* death: we'll be ridiculed, exposed, bankrupted or depilated, unless. . . The techniques are so similar, with sudden reversals, intense suspense relieved by false security, and that moment when life becomes absolute bloody — or hilarious — nightmare. In horror shows, we walk barefoot in lava; in farce, we skate on hot ice.

For us, theatre at its best is this art extremes. It's all, finally, about survival caught between warring gods, the salesma been dumped, the magician marshaling th his tempest-blown isle, the clown placating the giant firecracker. That firecracker may be entirely in our minds, yet we flap madly around center ring to escape.

These acts are a chronicle of that flap. This collection contains relatively few major deaths, but we hope the pieces carry the same threat (and promise) as longer work. For both writer and actor, a ten-minute sketch requires the discipline of haiku. Establish real characters in about one minute flat. Space the laughs or winces. Find one vivid image, one strong twist and punch. Avoid fishing for laughs with any cheap bait — there's nothing worse than forcing the audience into live canned laughter. And then, after all your technical expertise, revision and rehearsal, do your damndest to make it *almost* fail, to take that over-the-top double loop and come near dumping the riders out. Otherwise it's like mounting the scariest roller coaster when the motor's off. The risk is what it's all about.

The first of the collection, **Peace Negotiations**, is our most recent. It stemmed from a half hour of watching two elderly women in downtown Allentown, Pennsylvania, nurse their sore feet while straining to decipher the Burger King menu. In its first staging, the actresses tended toward old-age caricature. But as they began to focus on physical realities — their shoes, purses, the choreography of packages, their money-saving coupons, the blur of the menu board — they gradually began a sweet journey into the surprisingly alien world of the familiar.

As playwrights, we start with what itches. Why have we kept this absurd news article? Why on earth do we chuckle whenever we see that pathetic man? Why was that nice woman's comment so disturbing? Then we search implacably for the flea.

— C. Bishop & E. Fuller
November, 1989

PEACE NEGOTIATIONS

> *Two old ladies, laden with shopping bags and packages, totter into the Burger King.*

MAG
There.

MOO
Where?

MAG
By the wall.

> *They sit heavily. Long business of disencumbering themselves of packages, putting them on the table, restacking them on the floor. When everything is arranged at last:*

MOO
Maybe we better move.

MAG
How come?

MOO
I don't know if they allow you to sit. Maybe they set you where they want you.

MAG
It's a Burger King. You sit where you want.

MOO
Some places they make you sit where nobody sees. If they think you downgrade the clientele.

MAG
They don't have clientele. It's a Burger King.

> *They adjust themselves.*

I didn't mean to make you mad.

MOO
I wasn't mad.

MAG
You got pretty mad.

MOO

I don't get mad. I got high blood pressure, so sometimes I turn red.

MAG

You called me names.

MOO

What names?

MAG

You called me a f-a-r-t.

MOO

I was just stating a fact.

They adjust themselves.

MAG   BEAT

We better order.

MOO   STANDS

I'll order. I'm gonna pay for it.

MAG

No you're not.

MOO

I am. What do we do?

MAG

We decide what we want, then we go up there to the
counter.

MOO

If we're both up there, somebody's gonna sit here.
The government's bringing in all these refugees.

MAG

Then you go up and order, then come back, and then
I'll go up and order. Then we both pay for our own.

MOO

Not if I say so.

MAG

You think you'll spend a buck and get on my good
side.

MOO

You don't have a good side.

MAG
I don't get stuff like this from my other friends.

MOO
You don't have any other friends.

MAG
I value the freedom.

Silence. βεατ

I'm going to have a hot dog.

MOO
If they have it.

MAG
They have to have a hot dog. They're competing for customers. They'll sell you whatever your heart desires. They'll sell you a burger on a stick. They'll sell you a toasted cat. They got thousands of people, night and day, devoted to figuring what you want.

MOO
They have no idea.

MAG
Well I want a hot dog.

MOO
Then you better go get it.

MAG
I wasn't trying to make you mad. I was offering sympathy. Try do some good in the world. I read an article, "What My Retarded Sister Taught Me About Life." Made me wish my sister was retarded.

MOO
You better shut up on the subject.

MAG
I'm not saying a word. How do you feel?

MOO
If you wanta know, I feel like death warmed over.

MAG
Well check the menu.

Moo stares at her.

I was telling a joke.

MOO
Some patriot said to George Washington? "I regret
that I have one life." That's how I feel.

MAG
They don't believe in Washington or Lincoln any
more.

looking for hope

MOO
No, it's just the hope. Just not having the hope.

MAG
That he might show up some time?

MOO
Not any more.

MAG
We better order. They'll call the cops on us. Come
in with police dogs. I'm hungry.

MOO
Have to see what's on the coupons.

MAG
I don't need a coupon.

MOO
We got'em, we better use'em.

MAG
I don't have any.

MOO
I got these two-for-ones. If you don't use it, I can't
use it. It takes two.

MAG
This ain't a two-for-one.

MOO
No, this is. But this, ok, you can get a cheeseburger,
and if you get a cheeseburger, then you get fries and
a medium coke.

MAG
I don't want that.

MOO
Well there's that. Or you get cole slaw if you get the
bacon double cheeseburger. That comes with soup.

MAG

I'd rather have soup. I don't want the bacon.

MOO

You have to have the bacon. If that's the deal. They have it worked out so they make a profit and they give you a good deal. You both have to play the game. If you want something else, then don't complain if you get it.

MAG

Why can't I have what I want?

MOO

Cause we got the coupons for this.

MAG

I'm paying for my own.

MOO

I don't want you to. I want to treat you.

MAG

It's no treat if it's not something I want.

MOO

It's a treat when I say it is!

MAG   explota

You're nuts! You're trying to start something cause you feel sorry for yourself. You should be ashamed. You're not alone. You got friends, they brought over their cat. You're in the hospital, you got a ton of flowers, I come to visit there's no place to sit, I felt like a weed. You got no reason to act like that. You didn't care nothing about him when he was alive. You hadn't seen him in eighteen years, you told me, he treated you like dirt. You done all right without him, didn't you? So now you'll do all right without him some more. Look at all the stuff you bought.

MOO

I'm hungry.

MAG

So am I.

MOO

Shut up and let's eat. What else they got?

MAG
Well they got the Fun-Pak. Hamburger and fries
and a coke. It comes in a funny box.

MOO
That's for little kids.

MAG
I think you can have it if you want.

MOO
They don't call it a Fun-Pak if they think old ladies
buy it.

MAG
Old ladies can have fun.

MOO
Name one.

MAG   *STANDS*
We have to go up and order. Else we sit here and
starve.

MOO
You order first. I'll wait.

MAG
You can't just sit and starve.

MOO
Millions do. Ethiopia. Sit there and starve.

MAG   *SITS*
They don't sit in a Burger King.

MOO
You having a good time?

MAG
Yes. Are you?

                No response.

You are and you just don't know it.

MOO
I have to see what I bought.

MAG
Don't you know?

MOO
Nothing I need.

MAG
You're just full of sunshine.

MOO
What really hurts. . .

Near tears, controls herself.

What hurts is I never saw him get old. He was always young, and I knew he had his women, but I
knew we'd get old together. Then he takes off, and I
threw all his stuff in the trash, every damn thing.
But stuff keeps turning up. Old shirt stuffed down
in the paint cans. Ashtray from Yellowstone. Junk
mail for eighteen years. And then a letter. "Hello,
I'm your ex-husband's daughter. He's dead. Best
wishes." It hurts to get the damn comfort. It hurts
there's nothing left to want. I wake up early morning, it's too early to get up, there's nothing to do, but
you can't crawl back into your dream. I buy all this
trash so I got something to carry around, and all I
got to sit and talk is an old blubbery fart like you.

Mag considers a while, makes a fart sound.

MAG
I said I was sorry for you.

MOO
Yes you did.

MAG
Well I'm not.

MOO
Ok.

MAG
That make you feel better?

MOO
No.

MAG
At least you got me.

MOO
Ok.

MAG
Didn't want to make you mad.

MOO
No.

MAG
There's a time for everything. Time for laughing
and a time for crying—

MOO
They say so—

MAG
Time for shopping, time for staying home—

MOO
That's right—

MAG
And a time for eating lunch.

MOO
I'm not very hungry.

MAG
No.

MOO
It's not so easy to figure the ins and outs. There
used to be waitresses once.

MAG
That was another time.

MOO
That was a better time.

MAG
It seems like, now.

MOO
It didn't then.

MAG
You never had him. You just had a coupon that said
you did. Told you the terms of the deal.

MOO
You had to have the burger when all you wanted
was soup.

MAG
He was some burger.

MOO
Raw.   *BEAT*

> *They laugh, take hands. Then they*
> *defocus, as if it never happened.*

We better head for the bus.

MAG
Don't you want nothing to eat?

MOO
I'll fix some coffee.

MAG
You said you were starving.

MOO
Well I thought you were gonna eat.

MAG
Not if you don't.

MOO
It's too complicated. I think my feet are better now.

MAG
I'm ready when you are.

MOO
We still have to pay.

MAG
We'll pay for our own.

MOO
It's my treat.

MAG
I said no.

MOO
Like it or not.

MAG
I said no!   *CA   AGARYKA*

> *The quarrel is about to escalate. Pause.*
>   *BEAT*

We never ate.

MOO
So we don't have to pay.

MAG
We already paid.

> *They rise, pick up packages, helping one*
> *another load up. They stand a moment,*
> *balancing each other. Mag starts out,*
> *halts. Moo turns back to table.*

MOO
I'm gonna take some sugar.

> *She picks up a handful of packets. They go*
> *out.*

Part One
BARBED ENCLOSURES

These four acts are about all our favorite forms of entrapment: barbed enclosures we're tossed into, or apply to inhabit, or tolerate because, despite the stuffiness and the squawk of the smoke detector, things look even worse outside.

All present the actor with a special problem directly linked with their metaphors. While two (**Miss Bleep** and **Factory Dance**) are staged with characters faced directly front and the other two (**Dalmatian** and **Tell It Like It Is**) are played across a desk, all four have an unspoken orientation to *what's out front*. While the characters never speak to us, the audience, or ever really acknowledge their stage isolation, their atmosphere is fraught with an underlying sense of Something Outside. It's as if they see in their peripheral vision the monster's huge, glowing eyes in the west wall, as if they have an overwhelming urge to look directly at that blurred terror, yet can't. In all, these characters are more acutely aware of the brooding presence of the observer than of their partner's reality. This is the heart of their loneliness.

So in each, the actor should start with the question, "What's the story about?" The stylistic choices themselves are part of the meaning. If a direction reads, "He speaks to the audience," the question is *Why?* What is "the audience" for him? What creature is he reaching for? Does he anticipate love, hostility, understanding? Can he *see* the creatures in front of him, or does he face a bank of blinding lights?

These acts don't contain "asides" as later ones do, but it may be helpful to think of the characters *wanting* to speak directly to us and having to cope with that jolt when their minds re-enter the story. How do they respond to that moment? Terror, relief, embarrassment at having been absent? And when one responds to an on-stage partner, how does that looming presence of the audience affect the transaction? How does it feel to make love or have a horrible, humiliating fight in front of the TV cameras, the crew and a thousand other people, and have to pretend you don't see them?

Miss Bleep generated from a Theatre X improvisation in 1970 and was then scripted, taking a firm spot in the **X COMMUNICATION** repertoire for the next three years, with few changes other than ad lib expansions, the shifting tonalities of cast rotation, and at one point the startling image of a Miss Bleep who was 8 months pregnant. In 1985, we resurrected it for a new Independent Eye revue, **Dreamers**, rewriting to sharpen the logical non sequiturs and the divide-and-conquer technique of keeping the students in line. A further adaptation was made in 1988 for our **Want Ads** radio series. A few notes based on this history:

* The students are fully adult, though with the juvenile moments that adults often have. They're not unlike the inmates of a women's prison at which we performed: grown women, many with horrific past lives, regressed to pre-teen behavior, like a drugged, hysterical summer camp.

* Miss Bleep is best played with few distinctly robotic features. She's a pleasant, though stationary, elementary school teacher: highly intelligent, severely brain-damaged. There are bugs in her programming, but it's not her fault.

* The characters are self-contradictory in the extreme. Here too, we've seen this most clearly in convicts we have known: warm, intelligent and caring one moment; self-destructive, stupid and mean the next. The students do have genuine cameraderie, and we should feel empathy with each; yet they can shift at a moment's notice to being each other's worst enemies. They're trying to survive.

* It's ironic that this fight for survival is minute by minute. This is the key to timing. The strongest moments are the dead halts in utter confusion, frustration or rage. Sometimes the character scrambles quickly to a new ploy, sometimes the seconds stretch to excruciating length; but always the sequences build to these pain centers. Those moments hold the meaning.

These pieces should be played for reality. They're intended to be funny, but the audience may or may not laugh, depending perhaps on the decor of their own personal four walls. The job is to make the contradictions vivid. Sadly, there are no lighted exit signs here. We recommend that as a task for the real world.

MISS BLEEP

A classroom. Four chairs in a row facing front, the third empty. Three persons, fully adult, sit as students, trapped in school in perpetuity. Behind, a computerized teacher stands: Miss Bleep.

BLEEP
AND NOW CHILDREN AS OUR LAST PROBLEM FOR TODAY WE HAVE TWO PLUS TWO EQUALS FOUR.

DUFF
Did you know that?

CINDY
Course I know that. I've known that for thirty years.

BLEEP
NOW CHILDREN PRESS THE WHITE BUTTON AND REPEAT: TWO PLUS TWO EQUALS FOUR.

DUFF
Oh for—

BLEEP
NUMBER TWO?

DUFF
Two plus two equals four Miss Bleep sir.

BLEEP
VERY GOOD NUMBER TWO BUT YOU MUST WAIT FOR THE OTHERS. NOW CHILDREN PRESS THE WHITE BUTTON AND REPEAT: TWO PLUS TWO EQUALS FOUR.

ALL
(mechanically) Two plus two equals four.

BLEEP
VERY GOOD CHILDREN BUT WE WANT MORE SPIRIT. TWO PLUS TWO EQUALS FOUR!!!

ALL
(with mock hysteria) Two plus two equals four!!!

BLEEP
VERY GOOD CHILDREN. NOW NUMBERS TIME IS
OVER AND IT IS TIME TO SPELL CAT. ARE YOU
READY? SPELL CAT NUMBER FOUR.

ARTIE
Is she serious?

DUFF
Shut up and answer the question.

BLEEP
SPELL CAT.

ARTIE
Ok. C-A-T. Cat.

BLEEP
SPELL CAT.

ARTIE
Cat. C-A-T.

BLEEP
SPELL CAT NUMBER FOUR.

ARTIE
(as she continues correcting) I did! C-A-T! That
spells CAT! C-A-T! Listen to me!

BLEEP
(simultaneously) SPELL CAT. SPELL CAT. SPELL
CAT. SPELL CAT.

ARTIE
Q-U-A-T-T!

BLEEP
I AM SORRY THAT IS NOT CORRECT. BUT THERE'S
ALWAYS A SECOND CHANCE. WOULD YOU LIKE A
SECOND CHANCE?

ARTIE
(taking a deep breath) Yeh. Ok. C-A-T.

BLEEP
VERY GOOD NUMBER FOUR. NUMBER ONE WILL
YOU TELL US ABOUT YOUR SUMMER VACATION.

CINDY
Well matter of fact I really had a wonderful summer
vacation—

BLEEP
I'M SORRY NUMBER ONE THAT IS NOT CORRECT.

CINDY
Well, huh? No, I really did—

BLEEP
THE CORRECT ANSWER IS THREE POINT ONE
FOUR. TELL US ABOUT YOUR SUMMER VACATION.

CINDY
Three point one four, Miss Bleep.

BLEEP
THAT IS A NUMERIC VALUE. PLEASE ANSWER
TEXT-ONLY.

ARTIE
Quit screwing around, will you?

CINDY
What am I sposed to do?

BLEEP
NUMBER THREE WILL YOU HELP NUMBER ONE?

Silence.

ARTIE
He ain't here, Miss Bleep.

BLEEP
NUMBER THREE?

CINDY
Miss Bleep, he's not here.

DUFF
One means there's a vacancy in the Three slot.

Ad lib: She continues repeating.

Don't you remember yesterday? Miss Bleep, yesterday he flipped. Number Three flipped.

CINDY
They took him away, Miss Bleep.

ARTIE
He blew his cool.

CINDY
Blew his cool? He blew his brains out.

ARTIE
Ah he was a creep.

BLEEP
I'M SORRY NUMBER THREE YOU HAVE A NEGA-
TIVE ATTITUDE. YOU WILL NOW RECEIVE THREE
SECONDS OF ELECTRONIC CORRECTION.   THIS
HURTS ME MORE THAN IT HURTS YOU.   THREE.
TWO. ONE. BEEEEEEEEEEEEEEEEEEP!

They sit watching the empty chair.

DUFF
Boy, he woulda felt that.

BLEEP
CHILDREN YOU MUST NOT HAVE A NEGATIVE AT-
TITUDE. YOU MUST HAVE A POSITIVE ATTITUDE.

ARTIE
Damn well better.

BLEEP
CHILDREN IT IS NOW MILK AND COOKIES TIME.
WHEN YOU HAVE PUT YOUR BOOKS AWAY YOU
WILL RECEIVE YOUR MILK AND COOKIES.

DUFF
She's in a helluva mood today.

CINDY
(pressing button) Miss Bleep?

BLEEP
YES NUMBER ONE?

CINDY
I really enjoyed Arithmetic Time today, Miss Bleep.
I really learned a lot.   You're a good teacher.

Others make kissing and slurping sounds.
She turns to them, in a bitter undertone:

Listen, jerks: I survive.

BLEEP
THANK YOU NUMBER ONE. WHAT IS YOUR NAME?

CINDY
Cindy.

BLEEP
THANK YOU CINDY. THAT'S A NICE NAME. ISN'T IT
A BEAUTIFUL MORNING CINDY?

CINDY
Very nice.

BLEEP
ISN'T IT A BEAUTIFUL MORNING CINDY?

CINDY
Really.

BLEEP
ISN'T IT A BEAUTIFUL MORNING CINDY?

CINDY
Three point one four, Miss Bleep.

BLEEP
THAT IS CORRECT NUMBER ONE.

DUFF
(pressing button) Bleep?

BLEEP
NUMBER TWO?

DUFF
I gotta go to the can.

BLEEP
NUMBER TWO?

DUFF
Yeh, number one and number two.

BLEEP
NUMBER TWO IT IS NOW TIME FOR MILK AND
COOKIES. IT IS NOT YET TINKY TIME.

DUFF
But I gotta go!

BLEEP
TO THE WHAT, NUMBER TWO?

DUFF
I have to go to the toilet, Miss Bleep.

BLEEP
TO THE WHAT?

DUFF
Restroom.

BLEEP
TO THE WHAT?

DUFF
(under duress) To the urinary depository.

BLEEP
TO THE URINARY DEPOSITORY WHAT?

DUFF
To the urinary depository *quickly*!

BLEEP
TO THE URINARY DEPOSITORY MISS BLEEP.

DUFF
"To the urinary depository, Miss Bleep!"

BLEEP
VERY GOOD NUMBER TWO. IT IS NOW MILK AND
COOKIES TIME.   NUMBER ONE YOUR DESK IS
OPEN. YOU MAY NOW RECEIVE YOUR MILK AND
COOKIES.

CINDY
Thank you, Miss Bleep.

> *She mimes lifting a restraining bar on her
> seat, goes to Bleep, who mimes dispensing
> milk in a paper cup, then cookies.*

My name's Cindy.

> *Receives an extra cookie.*

DUFF
Hey, what about me? I gotta go! This damn button
doesn't work. *(pushing Cindy's button)* I gotta go!

CINDY
Miss Bleep, he's pushing my button!

BLEEP
CHILDREN YOU ARE NOT ALLOWED TO PLAY WITH
YOUR BUTTONS. NUMBER ONE WHAT DO YOU SAY
FOR YOUR MILK AND COOKIES?

CINDY
Thank you, Miss Bleep. My name's Cindy.

BLEEP
YOU'RE WELCOME CINDY. YOU MAY NOW GO TO
THE URINARY DEPOSITORY.

CINDY
But I don't need to go, Miss Bleep. That was Number Two.

DUFF
It's me, Miss Bleep, I'm the one that has to go.

BLEEP
NUMBER ONE YOU MAY NOW GO.

CINDY
But I don't need to go, Miss Bleep. I couldn't do
anything.

BLEEP
NUMBER ONE YOU MUST NOW GO.

CINDY
I'll try. . .

Goes out.

DUFF
What the hell am I gonna do?

ARTIE
Why don't you shut up? I'm hungry. I want my
milk and cookies.

DUFF
(in muffled voice, pressing Cindy's button) Bleep? Dis
is duh Breather calling. Haaaah. . . haaaah. . . Oh
honey, lemme feel those electrons humming. . .

BLEEP
NUMBER ONE YOU ARE NOT USING THE RECOM-
MENDED VOCABULARY FOR YOUR AGE LEVEL.
YOU WILL NOW RECEIVE THREE SECONDS OF
ELECTRONIC CORRECTION.

Cindy returns and sits.

PREPARE FOR ELECTRONIC CORRECTION. THIS
HURTS ME MORE THAN IT HURTS YOU. THREE.
TWO. ONE. BEEEEEEEEEEEEEEEEEEEEEP!

Cindy, jolted by shock, shrieks.

CINDY
What did I do, Miss Bleep! I'm Cindy!

BLEEP
NUMBER TWO YOU MAY NOW RECEIVE YOUR MILK
AND COOKIES.

DUFF
Now listen, Miss Bleep, I really do not need milk
and cookies just right now, what I really need is to
go to the bathroom and—

BLEEP
NUMBER TWO YOU ARE BEING ANTISOCIAL. IF
YOU DO NOT IMPROVE I WILL PROVIDE ELEC-
TRONIC CORRECTION.

DUFF
(in a rush) Now wait, I got rights, this is a free
country, dammit, I'm a human being, I got basic
needs and nobody's got the right to—

BLEEP
THIS HURTS ME MORE THAN IT HURTS YOU.
THREE. TWO. ONE—

DUFF
No, wait, you don't wanna do that, I gotta—

BLEEP
BEEEEEEEEEEEEEEEEEEEEEEEEEEP!

> *Duff is jolted by extended shock. Pause.*
> *He realizes, looks, slowly uncrosses legs.*

CINDY
(giggling) He wet his pants.

BLEEP
NUMBER TWO YOU MAY NOW GET YOUR MILK AND
COOKIES.

ARTIE
Go on, why don't you get your milk and cookies?

BLEEP
NUMBER TWO YOU HAVE LOST YOUR TURN FOR
MILK AND COOKIES.

ARTIE
Wow, maybe she'll give me your milk and cookies.

BLEEP
NUMBER THREE YOU MAY NOW RECEIVE YOUR
MILK AND COOKIES.

ARTIE
There ain't no Number Three, Miss Bleep. I'm next.

BLEEP
HERE IS YOUR MILK NUMBER THREE. SHHHHHP!

Milk is dispensed down the drain.

ARTIE
Hey. . .

BLEEP
HERE ARE YOUR COOKIES NUMBER THREE.
CRRRRRRRRRRK!

ARTIE
Hey, crumbs! Wouldn't he go nuts!

BLEEP
NUMBER FOUR YOUR DESK IS OPEN. YOU MAY
NOW RECEIVE YOUR MILK AND COOKIES.

ARTIE
Thank you, Miss Bleep. O wow!

Lifts restraining bar, hurries up to Bleep.

Hey, there isn't any paper cups. Bleep, I need a cup.

BLEEP
HERE IS YOUR MILK, NUMBER FOUR. SHHHHHHP!

Milk is dispensed down the drain.

ARTIE
Hey, you poured my milk sploosh down the drain!

BLEEP
HERE ARE YOUR COOKIES NUMBER FOUR. CRK!
CRK! CRK! CRK!

ARTIE
Hey! These are crumbs. I want a cookie. I can't eat
a buncha crumbs.

BLEEP
NUMBER FOUR YOU MAY RETURN TO YOUR SEAT
WITH YOUR MILK AND COOKIES.

ARTIE

I don't have any milk and cookies! Crumbs I got.
Many crumbs do not a cookie make.

BLEEP

NUMBER FOUR YOU MUST RETURN TO YOUR SEAT.

ARTIE

Look, Bleep, you give extra to Number One and
then you give mine all to Number Three!

BLEEP

NUMBER FOUR THERE IS NO NUMBER THREE.

ARTIE

(skewered by the logic) Yeh, see— No— I mean—

BLEEP

NUMBER FOUR YOU MUST REGISTER YOUR PRO-
TEST THROUGH PROPER CHANNELS. THEN MISS
BLEEP WILL CONSIDER YOUR REQUEST.

ARTIE

Hell with that—

BLEEP

IF YOU DO NOT SIT THE OTHER CHILDREN WILL
RECEIVE ELECTRONIC CORRECTION.

ARTIE

Hey ho!

Others protest, enraged at Artie.

BLEEP

NUMBER FOUR YOUR FRIENDS WILL HELP YOU
RETURN TO YOUR SEAT.

ARTIE

Ok! Ok! But I better get those milk and cookies.

He sits down. The desk locks.

BLEEP

IT IS NOW NAPPY TIME. WHEN YOUR DESKS OPEN
YOU MAY GET UP AND GET YOUR BLANKETS.

ARTIE

Hey! Baloney on this Nappy Time. What about my
milk and cookies?

                    BLEEP
NUMBER FOUR YOU WILL FINISH YOUR MILK AND
COOKIES AND FOLD YOUR HANDS NEATLY ON
YOUR DESK.

                    ARTIE
But I don't got no milk and cookies to finish and fold
my hands on my desk!

                    BLEEP
NUMBER ONE YOUR DESK IS OPEN. YOU MAY GET
UP AND GET YOUR BLANKET.

                    Each in turn lifts the restraining bar,
                    mimes spreading rug on the floor, and lies
                    down awkwardly for a nap.

                    ARTIE
Listen, I can't eat these things. This is what they
used to feed to the hostages—

                    BLEEP
NUMBER TWO YOUR DESK IS OPEN. YOU MAY GET
UP AND GET YOUR BLANKET.

                    ARTIE
Listen, doctors' reports have proven that cookie
crumbs are hazardous to your health—

                    BLEEP
NUMBER FOUR YOU WILL NOW RECEIVE—

                    ARTIE
Ok, I'm gonna eat'em! Ok!

                    Stuffs crumbs into mouth. Chokes.

                    BLEEP
CORRECTION—

                    ARTIE
Wait! I can't swallow this crap!

                    BLEEP
CORRECTION—

                    ARTIE
Hold on!

                    Coughing, choking, he tries to open desk.

BLEEP
CORRECTION—

ARTIE
Get me outa here!

BLEEP
BEEEEEEEEEEEEEEEEEEEEEP!

> *Artie is jolted by shock, emits one slight gag, freezes in mid-swallow. Pause.*

YOU MAY GET UP AND GET YOUR BLANKET.

> *Artie lifts restraining bar, holds a moment in breathless suspension, then keels over onto the floor.*

CHILDREN MISS GRUEL WILL NOW SING YOUR LULLABY. GET UP AND GET YOUR BLANKET NUMBER FOUR.

> *"Lullaby and good night," by scratchy recorded voice, continuing. Cindy and Duff, lying on the floor, look at Artie's body.*

CINDY
What's the matter with him?

DUFF
Shut up. Turn over. Don't look.

> *They turn over, settle into their nap. Lullaby continues.*

BLEEP
GET UP AND GET YOUR BLANKET, NUMBER FOUR.
GET UP AND GET YOUR BLANKET, NUMBER FOUR.
GET UP AND GET YOUR BLANKET, NUMBER FOUR.

> *Blackout.*

TELL IT LIKE IT IS

Office. A harried, balding man in a crumpled business suit searches his desk, then the floor under the desk. A neatly dressed woman appears hesitantly. He startles.

BOSS
Who are you?

FLORA
What?

BOSS
Whatta you here for?

FLORA
I was sent in. Flora Riddle.

BOSS
Oh, you're the one. Have a seat.

FLORA
Thank you.

They sit. He continues searching.

BOSS
(distractedly) So you been here two weeks?

FLORA
I started the day my divorce was final.

BOSS
Congratulations. So you like your job, the people you work with?—

FLORA
Well, it's hard to get acquainted, you know, always on the telephone—

BOSS
Like on coffee breaks, their throwing their coffee cups at the walls doesn't bother you?

FLORA
No, it takes a little getting— I think I'm getting along fine. Better than fine. Dandy.

BOSS
So there's a couple things—

FLORA
Oh I need some feedback, because this is my first
job in, let's see, eight, nine years—

BOSS
(still searching) I had a sack of peanuts—

FLORA
Nine. Since I was married. You know, when you
haven't used your talents you're really not sure if
you still have them, and now the children are in
school, and of course I do need the money, so I kind
of see a new horizon up ahead, but I know there'll be
lots of long, hard work—

BOSS
(staring at her) You know this is a business.

FLORA
Oh yes, I understand business. My husband was in
business.

BOSS
My father started this business. Simple. Tell It
Like It Is, Incorporated. There are a billion people
out there who are mad. They are livid, they are pur-
ple, fuming, itching, belching with rage. They want
to kill. They want to break heads. But they got one
problem. They're chicken.

FLORA
Or it could be perhaps—

BOSS
So they come to us, and for a modest fee, we commu-
nicate their message, by telephone, to the person
they wanta dump on.

FLORA
We "tell it like it is."

BOSS
Simple. "Hello, I have a message. Will you accept
it? Ok. You slob, a kiss from you is like eating a
live chicken. Thank you, goodbye." Hiring us is like
hiring a hit-man. It's humane because it's quick.

FLORA
My supervisor used the image of—

BOSS
It's impersonal. *(feeling)* Aggh, they're down in the lining. Peanuts. I'm trying to stop smoking.

FLORA
Oh that terrible yearning—

BOSS
(chewing) My wife says I gained twenty pounds.

FLORA
Oh, you're married!

BOSS
Fifteen years.

FLORA
I would have thought you the carefree bachelor.

BOSS
I'm not exactly the type.

FLORA
My husband was like that. He was married but it didn't show.

> *At last, preliminaries done, he explodes,*
> *waving papers.*

BOSS
Mrs. Riddle! Mrs. Riddle, what is this? Here is a call to Boston, a three-minute message, you were on for an hour and a half. What are you doing on that phone?

FLORA
Calling.

BOSS
Don't get smart with me. Are you trying to drive me out of business? What is this?

FLORA
That is a telephone bill. We all get telephone bills.

BOSS
You talked an hour and a half person-to-person to that person.

FLORA
He couldn't understand the message.

BOSS
For an hour and a half he couldn't understand the
message?

FLORA
He kept saying, "I don't understand, I can't understand it." He really needed to talk.

BOSS
Well he can talk to the wall, not to you. You're not
paid to listen, you don't have a license to listen,
you're not a professional nut-farmer. *(checking file
folder)* You're doing about fifteen calls a day. Even
our dumb girls can handle forty calls. You're fired.

FLORA
Well, could I ask a few questions?

BOSS
Look at these transcripts. You say, "Hey, I have
this message, but it's kind of mean, are you sure you
want to hear it?"

FLORA
I was trying to make it not so depersonalized.

BOSS
"Hey, it's ok, she didn't mean that. You really
sound like a nice person."

FLORA
He was crying.

BOSS
This isn't the job for you.

FLORA
You know, I don't think you realize what you have
here. All these telephones. It's like little fingers
reaching out all over the globe, and there are so
many people out there who ought to have a lot more
phone calls.

BOSS
(the final word) But not from you. Not on my
phones. You're fired. Get out.

FLORA
I have just one question.

BOSS
What?

FLORA
Does your wife work?

BOSS
(confused) Yeh, she's an RN at the hospital.

FLORA
Why then she could help with your smoking! You should just level with her.

BOSS
Didn't I just fire you?

FLORA
Well you weren't really that definite.

BOSS
Ok. Ok. Ok. Try again. You have a message. It's laying over here in a pile on the right. You take it—

FLORA
Let me point out one thing. It's easier for me to take it from the left.

BOSS
You take the message. Read it. Hang up. Simple. Wanta try? Here's one. Use my phone. Dial nine.

FLORA
Oh, I really appreciate. . . *(dialing)* You know, I can take criticism, I have a lot of previous experience with criticism. . . I dialed my own number. Sorry. *(dialing)* You know I just felt I should give a little more, there's so much alienation. . . Dial nine. *(dialing)* But I can adapt. . . This phone, is this a left-handed phone? It's ringing! Hello? Hello, Mrs. Marie Schwartzberg? This is Tell It Like It Is, we have a message, will you accept it? No, there's no charge, it's prepaid—

Pause. To Boss:

She has to turn off the stove. I always get caught like that—

To phone:

All right? Do you know a Tom? This says "Sincerely, Tom." Oh, your husband? Ex-husband? Well, so
am I, as a matter of fact. No, but I'm getting off the
track. All right, the message is—

Pause. To Boss:

The baby's crying. See, because I do have commu-
nications skills and I think a real knack for working
with people—

To phone:

Hi, there. Ok. The message is, "Marie, you take
your—" Do you mind a little obscenity? Like
damn? Oh. Hey that's pretty good! "Hell no!" she
says. Ok. "You take your damn goldfish and fry
them for Sunday dinner. Sincerely, Tom." That's
the message.

BOSS
Hang up.

FLORA
I have to hang up now. Is that all right?

Listens. Upset:

Hey listen. . . Do you *have* goldfish? Two fish and a
baby. Why doesn't he like the goldfish?. . . Oh,
they're not goldfish? Japanese fighting fish? Well
then how observant is he then really? Now I don't
know how you feel about it, but I don't really think
he has his hat on straight, so to speak—

BOSS
Hang up the phone.

FLORA
No, but she's just beginning to handle it. *(to phone)*
You know, my husband was the same way, of course
he— So did mine! The old seven-year itch. Only he
was a little slower, more like the ten-year itch. But
he still is able to really hurt me sometimes, something about the children, maybe— Oh yes, I have
children, not goldfish. Fighting fish. Fighting children! *(laughing)* Well, I think you ought to cook up
a *huge* fish dinner and send him the tails!

Listens.

Well, I've enjoyed. . . Wonderful! Well I'm glad! Sometimes things start out terrible and. . . Well, you've done the same for me. Bye.

> *She hangs up. Looks at Boss. He shakes his head.*

            BOSS

Well, Mrs. Riddle. We're looking for the type of person that doesn't really give a damn. That's why we prefer a college graduate.

> *Silence. She stands.*

Nothing personal. Ok? You upset?

> *No response.*

Like you really want to tell me off, but you think you might blubber?

> *No response.*

But you gotta do something or it's really gonna be bad. So we got these standard messages for getting fired. Send me one of those, I'll call myself and tell me what a jerk I am, ok? We'll bill you.

> *She goes out.*

I hate peanuts.

> *He chews. Blackout.*

These sit-at-a-desk sketches make nervous actors nervous. They should be played realistically, but that doesn't mean adding furniture or allowing actors to sit, stand, and walk around stage merely in order to present difficult moving targets to the viewers. In real life, people trot about far less than actors normally do on stage: we've personally had night-long kitchen quarrels totally devoid of stage movement other than pounding the wall, yet a hidden observer would have found them very expressive. Crucifixions drew large, appreciative crowds, despite poor choreography. The characters in these acts are spiked into their realities.

And despite the farce extrapolation, this work is a compendium of debris from the so-called real world. We can empathize with the lady in **Tell It**, but when her twin sister worked in our theatre's office, we reluctantly found ourselves playing the other role. Like a friend of ours, though his world is shrinking to the contents of a peanut sack, the Boss can't let go of a business he hates: it's his legacy. The sketch drew also on the schizoid experience of having to fire someone, while recalling vividly the shock of having once been fired for doing not a bad job but, worse, a *wrong* job.

Dalmatian evolved from an improvisation at a church workshop in Illinois about a woman's dim recollection of having been accused of student plagiarism, a story later told us, with variants, on four separate occasions. "I'll take the dog, you can have the kid" came from a Dear Abby letter. The "ten-thirty bell" story was the true experience of a residential care nurse in Baltimore. And while originally written for a male assistant principal (still playable that way), casting an actress in the role required adaptations that drew on the experience of friends desperate to escape dead-end jobs. It's comedy of grim recognition.

But for the characters, it's no laughing matter. The sketches lack both clowns and villains; or rather, they lack participants willing to play those roles. They simply chronicle the limp everyday atrocities people commit on one another, each claiming the role of victim while just trying to survive. None of these people are any less bright than the actors who play them, and none have the actors' envied advantage: nobody's written a script for them, and they can't exit their roles once their act is done. They're doing their best, though their best is pretty bad.

DALMATIAN

Mrs. Leonard, an assistant principal, sits at desk, talking on the phone as she processes a stack of papers.

MRS. LEONARD
Yes, well I'm sorry, Mrs. Bennett, but we do have state guidelines. If your son hasn't attended classes for the last eight months then I really doubt he's ready to graduate. No, Mrs. Bennett. Our guidelines require that ninth graders be reading at least at the sixth grade level and our seniors at least at the third.

Kathy, a student, appears.

Come in. *(on phone)* Then I suggest you call the principal and tell him what you think of me.

Hangs up.

What can I do for you?

Ceremonial reflex, just going through the motions: Mrs. Leonard stands, Kathy kneels, covers head with schoolbooks.

KATHY
Miss Henderson sent me.

MRS. LEONARD
Oh. Kathy. Have a seat.

She sits, consults a folder. Kathy sits in the chair opposite.

Let's see. You were here once before. Mr. Bilsing—

KATHY
Mr. Bilsing doesn't like me.

MRS. LEONARD
"Disturbing the class."

KATHY
He got real snotty and I started to cry, and he said that disturbed the class.

MRS. LEONARD
Well, now it's Miss Henderson.

Phone rings.

Excuse me. *(answering)* No, I can't take a call now, Phyllis, I've got a student. Who is it, a parent? That's ridiculous. There is no drug problem at this school. His daughter will have absolutely no problem getting any drug she wants.

Hangs up. Reflex: stands as Kathy kneels.

What can I do for you?

KATHY
Miss Henderson sent me.

MRS. LEONARD
Oh, Kathy. Have a seat.

They sit.

Now what is this? It says you were arguing with a teacher in a loud, abusive tone of voice.

KATHY
She was arguing with me.

MRS. LEONARD
About a poem.

KATHY
We had to write a poem. It said, "Write a poem based on a past experience in your life with deep emotional content using the rhyme scheme ABAB."

MRS. LEONARD
So?

KATHY
So I wrote the stupid poem. And she gave me an F.

MRS. LEONARD
Well, Kathy, perhaps if you'd read the instructions more carefully—

KATHY
So I ask her, "Why did I get an F, because it all rhymes, I mean." And she says, "Kathy, I cannot pass you on this because you obviously did not write the poem."

MRS. LEONARD
Well, that is a very serious accusation—

KATHY
She says, "You are a C student and this is an A
poem. And I know you copied it because I remember reading it somewhere." And I said, "But I did, I
did write it, and I didn't even babysit on Friday, and
I had a lot of trouble trying to rhyme some of the
words, like DALMATIAN."

MRS. LEONARD
Dalmatian?

KATHY
We had a dalmatian.

MRS. LEONARD
So?

KATHY
(reluctantly) When my mom and dad broke up, they
had this big fight about who got the dog, and finally
my dad says, "I'll take the dog, you can have the
kid." Dog was a dalmatian.

Phone rings.

MRS. LEONARD
Excuse me. (answering)   Phyllis, I said no calls! A
what? A bomb threat? They want the Principal. I
am the Assistant Principal, as you know. I handle
discipline, counseling, attendance, food service and
absurdity. The Principal handles fire drills. Bomb
threats come under fire drills.

Hangs up. Reflex: stands as Kathy kneels.

What is it?

KATHY
I'm Kathy-have-a-seat.

MRS. LEONARD
Oh yes. Have a seat.

They sit.

Kathy, my concern with you in this office is that you
were arguing with the teacher. Now if your interest
is poetry—

KATHY
I don't know that stuff. Last thing was on haiku. I
got a C on that—

MRS. LEONARD
Then you can find a time when she could sit down
and tell you everything you want to know about
poetry. She is a very good teacher, she can help you
write good poems, it's a good way to express yourself. Hollering at people is not a good way to
express yourself.

> *Phone rings. She answers, near shouting.*

Hello! Yes! No! No! Yes! No! Ok! Bye!

> *Hangs up. Reflex: starts to stand, halts,*
> *sits. Silence.*

Now Kathy. I'm sure that Miss Henderson has read
a great many poems, and she would certainly be
qualified—

KATHY
And she said it was good. *(realizing)* I wrote a good
poem. . .

MRS. LEONARD
Kathy, you know it is possible that at one time you
yourself read this poem—

KATHY
(mortally offended) I don't read poems!

MRS. LEONARD
And then you forgot it, and when you were writing,
it re-emerged from your subconscious.

KATHY
Huh?

MRS. LEONARD
It was in your subconscious.

KATHY
No, but we're Catholic.

MRS. LEONARD
I mean you didn't realize it, but the poem had
already been written, so in a sense you were correct
and Miss Henderson was also correct.

KATHY
When my dad left, he took the dalmatian. Two days later he came back, and I thought he was coming home, but he came back for the Alpo.

MRS. LEONARD
I don't care about the Alpo.

KATHY
It's in the poem! Does everybody's dad come back for the Alpo?

MRS. LEONARD
All right, but your test scores are below average in Verbal Synthesis. Not that we're trying to classify you—

KATHY
You *are* classifying me! Isn't it classifying me if I never wrote a poem before and now I write one and you classify that I can't?

MRS. LEONARD
We don't classify you for the sake of classifying you. We classify you so that we have more time to devote to your best interests.

KATHY
My best interests is that I wrote it. I wrote it. I WROTE IT, I WROTE IT, I WROTE IT!

Mrs. Leonard stands, Kathy kneels.

I really did.

Slowly, they sit again.

MRS. LEONARD
(*distractedly*) Kathy, the issue is not the poem. The issue is cooperation. The poem is not for the sake of the poem. The poem is experience in cooperation, fulfilling assignments, following directions. . .

She runs out of words. Long pause.

KATHY
(*frightened*) Mrs. Leonard?

MRS. LEONARD
Does any of this . . . make . . . any . . . sense?

KATHY
Uh-uh.

*Long pause. Mrs. Leonard takes off her
glasses, then speaks with quiet resignation:*

MRS. LEONARD
When I first came to work here, there was a bell
that rang at ten-thirty. Now that wasn't for classes
to change. Nothing happened at ten-thirty, except
that the bell rang. So I asked, "Why does that bell
ring at ten-thirty?" And I was told that it was the
Ten-Thirty Bell. And that we had always had a
Ten-Thirty Bell. And that it was not my position to
question the Ten-Thirty Bell. It took me some time
to get used to the fact that we had a Ten-Thirty
Bell, I used to get very upset every morning about
ten twenty-five. But I came to see at last that it did
have a function. It brought us together. It rang,
and we all knew we were part of something that
nobody understood, nobody knew the purpose, nobody could possibly change, but we were ALL IN IT
TOGETHER. Do you follow me? I understand your
problem, I sympathize—

KATHY
Then will you tell Miss Henderson to give me a
grade? Cause I wrote it, and she says it's good—

MRS. LEONARD
(losing control) NO I WILL NOT! DON'T YOU UNDER-
STAND? ARE YOU SO STUCK IN YOUR OWN PIMPLY
LITTLE PROBLEMS THAT YOU DON'T THINK ABOUT
MINE? WE HAVE TEACHER STRIKES, ASSAULTS ON
TEACHERS, DISRESPECT FOR TEACHERS, AND I AM
NOT ABOUT TO INTERFERE WITH THE BEST JUDG-
MENT OF A TEACHER BECAUSE A C-MINUS STU-
DENT WROTE A POEM! WHAT ABOUT MY NEEDS?
WHO IS FILLING MY NEEDS? WHERE ARE MY
STROKES? WHERE ARE MY WARM FUZZIES?

*Phone rings. She answers, shouting into
the phone.*

HELLO!

KATHY
I don't need an A! Just anything!

MRS. LEONARD

(changing tone) Oh honey, hi. What are you doing out of bed? If you're sick, you stay in bed, otherwise you go to school. Now I told you not to call unless it's an emergency. What's wrong? . . . I don't know if there's peanut butter, you're nine years old, you can look. Honey, I'm busy! . . . What? The mailman came? Is there a letter? Massachusetts? Can you read it? What do they say?

Listens expectantly. Suddenly drained:

How many applicants? Rats. No, it's ok. It's just that Mommy thought she had a chance. Well no, we'll stay here another year. Now you get back in bed. Love you. *(laughing)* Ok. Bye.

Hangs up. Chuckles.

My little girl said, "My orange juice tastes angry." A child's view of the world is something very precious.

Abruptly, Kathy rushes out. Mrs. Leonard looks after her, then picks up the phone.

Phyllis, will you take my calls? I need a potty break.

Blackout.

Steel traps are itchy themes in a society that advertises the absence of traps. The frazzled fur-bearing animals of **Dalmatian** turn their rage into cramped elbow jabs at their own rib cages. If they tried to gnaw off their own trapped foot, they'd probably chew the wrong one. In **Factory Dance**, our hero doesn't quite achieve the creative self-expression of the terrorist, but he tries.

Factory Dance is the oldest sketch in our trophy case. In 1969, we compiled ad phrases into a litany of imperatives, began improvising with a lock-step work-crew timed to the phrases. Quickly, the boredom provoked revolt, which formed the story's spine. For two years, it was played as an improvisation — sometimes muddled, sometimes terrifying — by a cast of nine, most often with a towering ex-Marine, Dan Desmond, in the role of the tormented aggressor. Cast changes necessitated that at last it become Literature.

The version presented here reduces the cast to three, though more can be included, simply going into place, doing their jobs, ignoring the furor, and signing out. For casts willing to tackle it, a good start is to spend a full rehearsal doing *nothing* but the gestures, phrases, sometimes a bathroom break. Make it real.

Performed at the height of Vietnam protest, in an atmosphere of self-cannibalizing revolt, viewers were torn between empathy with the hero and with those he brutalized. One factory owner (an arts patron prior to that evening) expostulated about our perceived slanders on factory owners; but for us, it has little to do with factories as such. Alienation could beset the most committed theatre, as we discovered on a haggard 1973 Ohio college tour, most audiences expecting a comedy act. Playing to four people in the Rio Grande College gym — the booker having scheduled us during semester break to get a reduced price — we had to ask why we were doing this? Simple. For the money.

Revived by Independent Eye in 1984, **Factory Dance** aroused only confused distaste for a tactless looney: Why watch the ravings of a guy we'd never invite to dinner? But we might look on the positive side: at least he didn't bring an assault rifle . . . this week. Each character is sentenced to solitary confinement, but every cell is crammed full, and this isn't the way we were told it would be.

FACTORY DANCE

*Amplified voice — short phrases, evenly
spaced, uninflected — continues unbroken.
Loudspeaker calls numbers.*

*As numbers are called, each person comes
into place. Positions of the three are stag-
gered in a nine-point square grid.*

*Each has a sequence of three gestures con-
tinually repeated, one to each phrase,
except when interrupted. Though gestures
are repeated endlessly, they're natural,
automatic but not robotic.*

*Carol (Six) does factory work, Margaret
(One) bookkeeping, Ric (Eight) sales.*

VOICE
Call your broker for more details.
See the Scramblers Three.
Call us now.
Save fifty cents.
Get fast relief.
Save nineteen cents.
Call Mister Stevens.
Pick your size and save.
See the Sweetheart Specials.

LOUDSPEAKER
EIGHT.

*Ric comes into place, up center. Begins ges-
tures as a salesman: smile, handshake,
relax.*

VOICE
Remodel now.
Get it all free.
Name this dog.
Get the best.
Beat the heat.
Go to bat.
Double your fun.
Eat and chew better.

LOUDSPEAKER
THREE.

*Ric watches an imaginary person taking
position down left.*

VOICE
Be enchanted by mink.
Run with Number One.
Use Desenex daily.
Discover our wide array.
Receive it free.

LOUDSPEAKER
ONE.

*Margaret comes into place, down right.
Begins work as bookkeeper.*

VOICE
Charge it.
Tell it like it is.
Say it with flowers.
Love it or leave it.
Let it soak in.

LOUDSPEAKER
TWO.

*Others look as an imaginary person takes
position down center.*

VOICE
Mix'em or match'em.
Let it be you.
Plug into real savings.
Take the Sudafed Challenge.
Act now.

LOUDSPEAKER
SEVEN.

*Ric watches an imaginary person take a
position to his right.*

VOICE
Put your dollars to work.
Give a damn.
See back of package for details.
Help carry the ball.

Save.
Hurry.
Blow yourself up.

>   LOUDSPEAKER
FOUR.

> *Imaginary person takes position right, be-*
> *hind Margaret.*

>   VOICE
Pick up a Dannon body.
Double your flavor.
Let it all hang out.
See surprising results.
Save seven cents.

>   LOUDSPEAKER
FIVE. NINE.

> *Imaginary persons take positions.*

>   VOICE
Pay nothing now.
See all the newest Fords.
Come and see.
See'em at Big George's.
Come see, come drive.
Come to our AMF ball-drilling jamboree.
Start looking around your home.
Shape your leisure time.

>   LOUDSPEAKER
SIX.

> *Carol takes a position left, begins gestures*
> *of an assembly line worker.*

>   VOICE
Shampoo with a full head of hair.
Ask us.
Just say Merry Christmas.
Save now.
Step into the future.
Sweeten the pot.
Smell terrific tonight.
Say Mister Hot Dog.
Buy one get one free.
Whip up a heap.

Look trim and slim.
Take a closer look.

> *Ric stops working, stretches. He watches*
> *the others continue, begins again, stops.*

Say no to pain.
Get it all free.
Save fifteen cents.
Remove unwanted hair.
Start with Finish.
Hug the Baggies Alligator.
Go for the gold.
Feel beautiful inside and out.
Attend the church of your choice.
Relax on a cushion of air.
Try us.
Prove it.
Call now.
Win big.
Pledge allegiance to value.

> *The phrases continue as he speaks.*

RIC

Hey, excuse me. Anybody got a
light? "Thanks, ok, where's the
fuse?" No, actually, does anyone
have change for a dollar? I need a
break. Anybody got change for a
dollar? Anyone got the time? How
bout some inside tips on the stock
market? . . . Ah, does anyone here
have hemorrhoidal discomfort? . . .
Hey, guys, is there anything I can
do for *you*?

> *No response. He tries to*
> *go back to work. Stops.*
> *Considers leaving. At*
> *last, he moves out of his*
> *space, going to others,*
> *real and imaginary.*

That's some job. Whatta you think
the weather's gonna do? They said
it was gonna clear up. I think they
must be doing something to outer

VOICE

Call your broker
for more details.

See the
Scramblers
Three.

Call us now.

Save fifty cents.

Get fast relief.

Save nineteen
cents.

Call Mister
Stevens.

Pick your size
and save.

See the
Sweetheart
Specials.

Remodel now.

Get it all free.

space. The Russians are shooting holes in the sky.

To another.

You know, I wish I knew a place to get a really good hot dog, I really love that. There's a new pizza place I found. That's really an art, you know, they oughta have art museums for pizzas. You got a cold, you oughta try Vitamin C.

To Carol.

Hey, I'm gonna get a cup of coffee, you want some?

No response. To another.

Hey, whatta you think about prayer in the public schools? I think we oughta pray *for* the public schools. Give'em some Vitamin C.

To another.

You know anything about palm-reading? I always wondered what I said.

To Margaret.

Did you see that article where the Air Force built this cannon to shoot naked chickens into airplane engines at 700 miles an hour? This is to see what happens when it hits a bird. But the question is, what does this do to the arms race? If we set up orbiting poultry farms and fire giblets down at the Commies. No, but there's great applications in consumer technology. Talk about fast food: Drive through Colonel Sanders, roll down the window, open your mouth, "I'd like two drumsticks." PKWWWWWWWW!

No response. To another.

Name this dog.

Get the best.

Beat the heat.

Use Desenex daily.

Discover our wide array.

Receive it free.

Charge it.

Tell it like it is.

Say it with flowers.

Love it or leave it.

Let it soak in.

Mix'em or match'em.

Let it be you.

Plug into real savings.

Take the Sudafed Challenge.

Act now.

Put your dollars to work.

Give a damn.

See back of package for details.

Help carry the ball.

Save.

Hurry.

Blow yourself up.

Pick up a Dannon body.

You don't know me personally, but
I do great backrubs. If you want a
backrub.

> *No response. He goes
> back to his position.
> Tries to work: smile,
> handshake, relax. Tries
> again. Stops. Considers
> a long time. At last, he
> breaks the pattern,
> addressing everyone:*

You know, I personally get very
upset myself if somebody kind of
makes himself a public spectacle
and disrupts things, cause everybody's got enough to worry about,
you don't want some jerk coming
along and violate your private
space. But I think what we really
want often is a sense that we are
really in touch with other people,
maybe somebody willing to take
what we have to give, and people
are really human, most of the time,
and maybe some friendliness, I
mean is the job really so important
that we can't take time to realize
that we are all on the same planet,
and we're all alive, and someday
we're all gonna die, so you might as
well have . . . a backrub.

> *Waits.*

I always wondered if I had one minute on national prime time and I
could say whatever I wanted to say,
what would I say?

> *He laughs. No response.
> He goes to Margaret, who
> continues her work.*

You know what I mean?

MARGARET

Yeh.

Double your
flavor.

Let it all hang
out.

See surprising
results.

Save seven
cents.

Pay nothing
now.

See all the
newest Fords.

See'em at Big
George's.

Come see come
drive.

Come to our
AMF
ball-drilling
jamboree.

Start looking
around your
home.

Shape your
leisure time.

Shampoo with a
full head of
hair.

Ask us.

Just say Merry
Christmas.

Save now.

Step into the
future.

Sweeten the pot.

Smell terrific
tonight.

Say Mister Hot
Dog.

Buy one get one
free.

Whip up a heap.

RIC
So whatta you think?

MARGARET
Yeh, it's a grind. Gets to you.

RIC
How's it get to you?

MARGARET
Same thing over and over. That's life.

RIC
You sure that's life?

MARGARET
Yeh I know. Scuse me—

RIC
What would you really like to do?

MARGARET
I'd like to go to Disneyland.

RIC
Wanta go right now?

MARGARET
Listen, I didn't get much sleep last night, and my eyes are giving me problems, I just got all this dumped on me which isn't my work but they cut back on the staff and they dump it on me, so—

RIC
Whyn't you tell'em go to hell?

MARGARET
Look, if you have life so easy you can talk like that, good for you, good for you, but don't rub my nose in it, ok? I got seniority, I got fifteen years on my pension, I got a grievance in to the union, they'd just love to have the excuse.

RIC
I just asked.

Look slim and trim.

Take a closer look.

Say no to pain.

Save fifteen cents.

Remove unwanted hair.

Start with Finish.

Go for the gold.

Get it all free.

Hug the Baggies Alligator.

Feel beautiful inside and out.

Attend the church of your choice.

Enjoy big savings.

Support the party of your choice.

Relax on a cushion of air.

Try us.

Pledge allegiance to value.

Call your broker for more details.

See the Scramblers Three.

Go to bat.

Double your fun.

Eat and chew better.

MARGARET
Maybe later, ok? I agree with
what you said. That's all very
true. I just—

RIC
Yeh.

Back to place.

Boy. Wow. Must be party time.
Some other planet.

*He goes back to place.
Tries one last time to
work: smile, handshake,
relax. Frustrated, gives
it up. Moves down to
Carol, determined.*

Nice day.

CAROL
I wouldn't know. It was dark when
I came in.

RIC
Yeh, daylight savings. Whatta you
think about that?

CAROL
Makes it a little lighter when I get
out.

RIC
How is it when you get out?

CAROL
Dark.

RIC
Well it gives you time to go out and
fool around, huh?

CAROL
Not much of that.

RIC
Hey, you ever wonder about this
job? Why you come in here every
day?

Be enchanted by
mink.

Run with
Number One.

Call us now.

Save fifty cents.

Get fast relief.

Save nineteen
cents.

Call Mister
Stevens.

Pick your size
and save.

See the
Sweetheart
Specials.

Remodel now.

Get it all free.

Name this dog.

Get the best.

Beat the heat.

Go to bat.

Double your fun.

Eat and chew
better.

Be enchanted by
mink.

Run with
Number One.

Use Desenex
daily.

Discover our
wide array.

Receive it free.

Charge it.

Tell it like it is.

Say it with
flowers.

CAROL

That's easy. I got my family to
feed. You gotta have a job to feed
your family, don't you?

RIC

Hey, but I mean isn't there something you really wanted to do when
you were a kid?

CAROL

I wanted to have a family.

RIC

Yeh, so you got one, huh?

CAROL

Yep.

RIC

Well. Say hi to the kids.

He goes back to his place,
watches them. Heatedly:

You have any idea how abnormal
this all is? What's that sposed to
be? *(mimicking a gesture)* Is that
part of the evolutionary cycle? Is
that what you live for? Let's look at
ourselves a minute, hey? Self-
knowledge. Know thyself. Do you
think while you're doing that, or
does your brain turn into bubble-
gum? What's it gonna get you? A
new TV? They don't show you on
TV. If you were on TV, they'd put a
laughtrack on it. "Mrs. Homer
Jones of Texarkana, Texas, couldn't
get the dirt off her little boy, so she
boiled him in Clorox." "Yaaaaaay!"

MARGARET

What is it, are you selling something? I don't understand what
you're doing.

RIC

Do you know what *you're* doing?

Love it or leave
it.

Let it soak in.

Mix'em or
match'em.

Let it be you.

Plug into real
savings.

Take the
Sudafed
Challenge.

Act now.

Put your dollars
to work.

Give a damn.

See back of
package for
details.

Help carry the
ball.

Save.

Hurry.

Blow yourself
up.

Pick up a
Dannon body.

Double your
flavor.

Let it all hang
out.

See surprising
results.

Save seven
cents.

Pay nothing
now.

See all the
newest Fords.

Come and see.

See'em at Big
George's.

MARGARET
I don't know.

RIC
You don't know anything.

MARGARET
Right, I don't know anything. This
isn't the time or the place.

CAROL
Just ignore it.

RIC
Ignore it. Ignore *it*? I'm an It.
We're all an It. *(at Carol)* Look.
It's working. It's got a purpose in
life. The highest aspirations of the
human soul. It's doing a dance.
They call it the Robot. It starts
each day with a hearty breakfast of
Froot Loops and Diet Pepsi and
then it keeps twitching all day till
it blows a tube—

CAROL
Ok, I'm a robot, I'm dumb, it's all
my fault, and I shoulda just
decided I was gonna be rich and
that's all it takes—

RIC
Tell me more.

CAROL
I'll tell you this. You're like a
spoiled little baby. You come in
here, you start yelling, hassling
everybody, and I'm sorry, you poor
child, but we are busy, and we are
tired, and I wish to God—

RIC
Don't blame it on God, lady—

CAROL
Look, you don't know me, you don't
know who I am, you don't know my
life, so what do you care?

Come see, come
drive.

Come to our
AMF
ball-drilling
jamboree.

Start looking
around your
home.

Shape your
leisure time.

Shampoo with a
full head of
hair.

Ask us.

Just say Merry
Christmas.

Save now.

Step into the
future.

Sweeten the pot.

Smell terrific
tonight.

Say Mister Hot
Dog.

Buy one get one
free.

Whip up a heap.

Look slim and
trim.

Take a closer
look.

Say no to pain.

Get it all free.

Save fifteen
cents.

Remove
unwanted hair.

Start with
Finish.

Hug the Baggies
Alligator.

RIC
I'm on the same planet as you, I
wanta know what it is makes you
tick, what makes you tick—

Mimicking.

Tick tick tick tick tick—

MARGARET
Let her alone!

RIC
Alone. She is alone. Look at her,
she is damned alone. I mean when
you fall in your grave what's the
good you spent all this time dancing
your little foxtrot?

CAROL
Because my children will be on this
earth after me!

RIC
And what will they be doing? The
same goddamn thing! I'm just asking WHY!

CAROL
Because we can't afford not to!

RIC
Hafta buy that new home entertainment center—

CAROL
I have to buy food and pay rent—

MARGARET
Just stop telling us a dozen times—

RIC
I'm not telling you anything—

MARGARET
Ain't it the truth.

CAROL
Why do you want to know? Do you
know my children? You don't even
know my children's names.

Go for the gold.

Feel beautiful
inside and out.

Attend the
church of your
choice.

Enjoy big
savings.

Support the
party of your
choice.

Relax on a
cushion of air.

Try us.

Prove it.

Call now.

Win big.

Pledge
allegiance to
value.

Call your broker
for more
details.

See the
Scramblers
Three.

Call us now.

Save fifty cents.

Get fast relief.

Save nineteen
cents.

Call Mister
Stevens.

Pick your size
and save.

See the
Sweetheart
Specials.

Remodel now.

Get it all free.

Name this dog.

RIC
Hey, they've got names!

Get the best.

Beat the heat.

CAROL
Yes they've got names! Why don't
you ask us our names? If you care
about us, why don't you even ask
us our names?

Go to bat.

Double your fun.

Eat and chew
better.

RIC
What's your name?

Be enchanted by
mink.

CAROL
What do you care?

Run with
Number One.

RIC
Oh God.

Use Desenex
daily.

*He gesticulates in help-
less, voiceless laughter.*

Discover our
wide array.

Receive it free.

Oh God. Tick tick tick tick tick—

Charge it.

CAROL
Stop it!

Tell it like it is.

Say it with
flowers.

RIC
Oh I don't mean to affect your
blissful existence—

Love it or leave
it.

Let it soak in.

CAROL
You're not affecting me in the least.

Mix'em or
match'em.

RIC
Great. Then you just do your job
and fall over dead for your kids—

Let it be you.

Just say Merry
Christmas.

CAROL
Just shut up about my—

Step into the
future.

Save now.

RIC
Go home and get laid and have
another kid so you got another reason to go to work—

Sweeten the pot.

Smell terrific
tonight.

CAROL
I can't have any more.

Say Mister Hot
Dog.

RIC
Sure you can! Do it the old-
fashioned way!

Buy one get one
free.

Whip up a heap.

CAROL
(snapping sharply) Because I can't
afford to have any more!

> *A hitch.*

RIC
That's not my point—

MARGARET
Why do you just go on and on—

RIC
And on and on and on and on—

> *Around to others.*

AND ON AND ON AND ON AND ON
AND ON AND ON AND ON—

> *Suddenly he stops,*
> *exhausted. Silence,*
> *except for phrases. Carol*
> *sobs, continues work dis-*
> *tractedly, mumbles to*
> *herself in dull pain:*

CAROL
I wanted a little girl . . . I lost my
little girl. . .

RIC
That's not the point. . .

CAROL
She was gonna be two. . .

RIC
The point I was trying to make. . .

CAROL
My little boy says, "Where's Mama
going?"

RIC
Yeh. . .

CAROL
"Don't go to work, Mama. . ."

RIC
That's cute. . .

Look slim and
trim.

Take a closer
look.

Say no to pain.

Get it all free.

Save fifteen
cents.

Remove
unwanted hair.

Start with
Finish.

Hug the Baggies
Alligator.

Go for the gold.

Feel beautiful
inside and out.

Enjoy big
savings.

Support the
party of your
choice.

Relax on a
cushion of air.

Try us.

Prove it.

Call now.

Win big.

Pledge
allegiance to
value.

Call your broker
for more
details.

See the
Scramblers
Three.

Call us now.

Save fifty cents.

Get fast relief.

CAROL
(losing control) I can't have any
more! I went to a goddamn cheap
doctor, and he screwed up my
insides, and now I can't ever have
any more!

RIC
Yeh look, the point I was making—
Look, you could sue'em— The
point I was—

Carol's sobs continue.

I just meant we oughta be human,
and figure out how to be more. . . I
mean this is an example, you—

Sobbing.

Stop it. Hey, that's a cop-out. I'm
not your problem, I'm the least of
your problems. . .

*Turning to the others,
desperately manic:*

Come on, let's have some answers
here. When do we get the answers,
for Christmas? Gonna tell me?
Tell me it's not so bad? Tell me
you're satisfied? Man, you better
not, cause the minute you're satisfied the economy stops dead. You
know that Libya is collecting enormous storage tanks of Coca-Cola?
There's a secret ingredient. It's a
fact. You know the Communists
are concealing the fact they've
already won? You know there are
countries where the children have
all disappeared? It's a fact. Come
on, now you tell *me* a fact. If you
know a fact, then tell me. If you
don't know, then tell me you don't
know. I want a beer I can die for. I
want just five minutes when all the
bullshit stops!

Save nineteen
cents.

Call Mister
Stevens.

Pick your size
and save.

See the
Sweetheart
Specials.

Remodel now.

Plug into real
savings.

Take the
Sudafed
Challenge.

Act now.

Put your dollars
to work.

Give a damn.

See back of
package for
details.

Help carry the
ball.

Save.

Hurry.

Blow yourself
up.

Pick up a
Dannon body.

Double your
flavor.

See surprising
results.

Pay nothing
now.

See all the
newest Fords.

Whip up a heap.

See'em at Big
George's.

*He runs dry. Looks
about, speechless, ges-
tures amorphously.*

MARGARET
You don't have my sympathy. You
don't have anybody's. Now you
know you can hurt somebody, huh?
You can make the lady cry? So?
You're still miserable. There are
people who are miserable because
they deserve to be. You gotta have
money before they'll give you a
loan, you gotta be loveable before
they love you. You won't get sympathy if anybody thinks you need it.
I can tell you that. There's just not
enough to go round.

RIC
(in an undertone) Tick tick tick
tick—

CAROL
Make him stop.

MARGARET
You know it's perfectly possible to
call the police—

RIC
Tick tick tick tick tick—

CAROL
I lost count—

RIC
Tick tick tick tick tick—

MARGARET
You'll have no effect at all, you'll
just disappear—

RIC
Tick tick tick tick tick—

MARGARET
You're just not part of this world!

Come see, come
drive.

Come to our
AMF
ball-drilling
jamboree.

Start looking
around your
home.

Shape your
leisure time.

Shampoo with a
full head of
hair.

Ask us.

Just say Merry
Christmas.

Save now.

Step into the
future.

Sweeten the pot.

Smell terrific
tonight.

Say Mister Hot
Dog.

Buy one get one
free.

Look slim and
trim.

Take a closer
look.

Say no to pain.

Get it all free.

Save fifteen
cents.

Remove
unwanted hair.

Start with
Finish.

Hug the Baggies
Alligator.

He stops. Silence, except for the phrases. Margaret continues working, Carol struggles to get back into the rhythm.

LOUDSPEAKER
THREE.

Ric looks up, watches an imaginary person go.

RIC
Look at that. I didn't go. She did. Call your number, that's it.

LOUDSPEAKER
FOUR.

Watches another.

RIC
Try five. How bout five?

LOUDSPEAKER
TWO.

Watches another.

RIC
Hey, where do they go? Potty break? Gas chamber? That's the way to solve unemployment. Just disappear.

LOUDSPEAKER
NINE.

RIC
Hey, old friend and neighbor. They oughta put a want ad. Wanted: just five minutes more.

CAROL
I'm so scared. I don't know why I'm so scared—

MARGARET
Shut up. Just do your job and just— Shut up.

Go for the gold.

Feel beautiful inside and out.

Attend the church of your choice.

Enjoy big savings.

Support the party of your choice.

Relax on a cushion of air.

Try us.

Prove it.

Call now.

Win big.

Pledge allegiance to value.

Call your broker for more details.

See the Scramblers Three.

Call us now.

Save fifty cents.

Get fast relief.

Save nineteen cents.

Call Mister Stevens.

Pick your size and save.

See the Sweetheart Specials.

Remodel now.

Get it all free.

LOUDSPEAKER
SEVEN.

Watches another.

RIC
Wanted: hope. New or used.

LOUDSPEAKER
SIX.

*Carol halts, stands a
moment, then goes off.*

RIC
Hey no. Where's she going? Hey.
Wanted: just one word or— Just
say hello. . .

LOUDSPEAKER
FIVE.

Watches another.

RIC
They just go. Is that what you do,
you just come and go? Send a sympathy card? Famous last words:
hello.

LOUDSPEAKER
ONE.

RIC
You got your pension?

*Margaret halts, goes off. He looks after
her, waves, then stands doing nothing.
Mumbles, mimicking phrases.*

VOICE
Love it or leave it.
Let it soak in.
Mix'em or match'em.
Let it be you.
Save now.
Step into the future.
Sweeten the pot.
Say Mister Hot Dog.

Name this dog.

Get the best.

Beat the heat.

Go to bat.

Double your fun.

Eat and chew
better.

Be enchanted by
mink.

Run with
Number One.

Use Desenex
daily.

Discover our
wide array.

Receive it free.

Charge it.

Tell it like it is.

Say it with
flowers.

Call us now.

Save fifty cents.

Get fast relief.

Save nineteen
cents.

RIC
Mister Hot Dog. . .

VOICE
Buy one get one free.
Whip up a heap.
Look slim and trim.
Take a closer look.
Say no to pain.

RIC
No. No pain. No pain.

VOICE
Get it all free.
Save fifteen cents.

> *He moves around the square aimlessly,*
> *starts to cry out, stops, frozen. At last, he*
> *returns to his place, stands, sticks out his*
> *hand. Tentatively, off-handedly, he begins*
> *work gestures again: smile, handshake,*
> *relax. Gradually, he begins to find security*
> *in the rhythm.*

Start with Finish.
Hug the Baggies Alligator.
Go for the gold.
Feel beautiful inside and out.
Attend the church of your choice.
Enjoy big savings.
Support the party of your choice.
Relax on a cushion of air.
Try us.
Prove it.
Call now.
Win big.
Pledge allegiance to value.

Blackout.

Part Two
FAMILY SLANDERS

The next four sketches represent types that have been immensely popular in performance, touring for years as part of our **FAMILIES** revue. While this show toured for many years, very little of its content was created with the theme of *families* in mind. Two of these acts were originally part of a show called **BLACK DOG**, a revue about anger as an integral part of our food chain; two others generated from sketches improvised by students at University of Delaware during residencies there, in shows entitled **KNOCK KNOCK** and its sequel **WHO'S THERE**. The greatest achievement of **FAMILIES** was its title: it was far easier to book a show called **FAMILIES** than one called **BLACK DOG**, and just about any subject would fit, by some stretch of the imagination. With audiences primed to look at the work for its close-to-home content, not just for its amusement value, they in fact did.

Though these acts all end in frustration and loss, audiences find them remarkably entertaining, perhaps because we all long for the validation of our trivialities. The Dutch bourgeoisie paid good money for genre paintings of their furniture, rugs, servants or fruit bowls; and we find comfort in the mere mention of the obvious facts that other people besides ourselves fight about taking out the garbage or getting a small kid out of a locked bathroom.

The danger here is to regard these people themselves as trivial, rather than as ordinary people living in the chilly bathroom of banality. There's little in the pieces that opens the characters' inner lives; they seem sprung from TV sitcom. This is a consequence of work being honed to specific performers: we depend on what others bring to it of their own quirky presence. Still, performers should keep in mind that while Ed and Bunny or Brad and Karyn strike us as being perhaps salesman and housewife, they could as easily be journalist and teacher, doctor and composer, social worker and playwright. The glitch in the pop-up toaster is the same for all, and the smoke of the wasted toast. Most of us act far more stupid than we actually are.

Nothing's directly at stake in these pieces except Happiness. All these families can afford to pay the gas bill. None is actually drinking, stealing cars or killing a wife with a crockpot. It's true that Love, Truth, and Responsibility are raped and left bleeding under the dinner table, but those aren't tangible commodities.

The greatest loss — what the actors must keep in mind constantly — is the characters' own faith that they have any power and control in their lives. The choice between Mickey Mouse and Donald Duck isn't a meaningful political option. Are the characters impelled to make the choices they do by what's ingrained in them? Of course. *Must* they make these choices? Absolutely not. Would *we* do the same shilly-shally? With a master's touch.

The sketches must get laughs; if they don't, the actors had best go home and pull down the blinds. But the laughter must rise from *recognition*. We need to hear our own voices speaking these outlandish absurdities: "Is that really what I sound like?" This sort of theatre gains its attractive danger from the simple fact of reflecting human behavior. It's not enough that the actors happen to be alive and not on celluloid: we have to feel that our own names are about to be called, and then all the dirty truth will come out.

But also, that we *share* this danger. None of us is exempt, by virtue of bank account, beauty, spelling medals or advanced degrees, from the common imperatives to digest, defecate, dance and die. It's a horribly forlorn feeling to see people — or even our own frail moments of forgettable daily life — vanish into the night. Friends have written us to share the small joys, the job layoffs, divorces, sibling simperings and major operations that are part of us as well as them, and somehow the unhappy news is as cheering as the cheerful: cheering in reminding us we're human and not entirely alone.

On the other hand, not being entirely alone means that we have extraordinary investment opportunities to make a mess of lives other than our own. Between "A little water clears us of this deed" and "What's done cannot be undone" lies a vast wasteland of human choice, a desert we stagger across in pitch black night, with flashlight batteries we bought last year on sale at K-Mart. Guaranteed.

HAPPY ANNIVERSARY

A celebratory dinner table. A couple sits gazing at one another. After a moment, they come alive, take hands, enraptured.

ED
Terrific meal.

BUNNY
For a terrific couple.

ED
Happy anniversary, Honey.

BUNNY
The first of many.

ED
Many happy returns.

BUNNY
Oh speaking of returns, you want to take a look at the bills?

ED
This is our anniversary, Honey—

BUNNY
There's a final notice.

ED
Yeh, but—

BUNNY
I'll put them on the desk.

ED
So many things have happened in one year. So many adjustments—

BUNNY
Adjusting, learning to give and take—

ED
Take charge of our lives, face up to those problems and solve them.

BUNNY
And now that we've solved them, it'll really be nice.

ED
Yeh, because it has been kind of rough, you know—

BUNNY
Sure, it's hard to grow. We've grown personally.

ED
We have. Like our quarrels have grown. I mean
they've matured.

BUNNY
And you know, when we have kids, I am never going
to be angry with them. It's just not necessary. If
you love them and raise them the right way, they'll
never cause you problems.

ED
Not many couples could say on their first anniversary they had solved all their significant problems.

BUNNY
But it's true.

ED
I think we're way ahead of most couples. Maybe
five years ahead of most.

BUNNY
Happy anniversary, Honey.

> *They lean across table, kiss. Then they
> turn front, speaking to us.*

Our marriage, well it's hard to talk about, because it
really has been this incredible experience—

ED
Incredible but believable. I mean we're more than
just married, we're good friends.

BUNNY
Course we're more than friends. It's so stimulating,
so liberating. I have been liberated to do so much.
New furniture, new colors, new recipes—

ED
Zulu cookery. We have so many tastes in common.
Even colors, I mean—

BUNNY
The brighter end of the chartreuse scale is not often
found—

ED
It's not often found so early in a marriage.

BUNNY
Really incredible.

> *They giggle, then turn to one another, hold-
> ing hands, laughing, playing with each
> other's fingers.*

Honey, before it gets too late and we get involved in
something else. . .

> *They giggle.*

Could you take out the garbage?

> *Dead silence.*

ED
Huh?

BUNNY
Could you take out the garbage? It's kinda piled up.

ED
Honey . . . You're gonna laugh.

> *He laughs.*

BUNNY
What?

ED
The garbage. I just can't . . . cope with the garbage.

BUNNY
Oh. Well, as long as it's out before breakfast.

ED
No, I don't mean garbage now. I mean garbage always. Garbage forever.

BUNNY
But we agreed. Garbage is your province. *(with
sudden concern)* Oh, are we making too much garbage. Is that it?

ED
No, it's not a recycling question, or less garbage or
better garbage. It's just the fact of garbage.

BUNNY
Well it's a human fact. We all generate refuse. If
you put two people together—

ED
That's it. That's it. This is our product. Our love,
our sensitivity results in this horrible accumulation.
Oh, I know it's a petty little thing—

BUNNY
Well it's not petty. There are three sacks of it. Honey, this is our anniversary. I would like it to be a
garbage-free anniversary.

ED
And how can we really, truly say Happy Anniversary when there is this external manifestation of
our relationship bulging across the kitchen at us?
The Johnsons, two doors down? He goes out once a
week with this little plastic thing, it doesn't look
like garbage, it doesn't act like garbage, it's a com-
pact but comprehensible concentration of semi-
organic substance, like the Johnsons. But ours—

BUNNY
I don't understand.

ED
Take out the garbage. Please. *You* take out the garbage.

BUNNY
Well. I could take out the garbage—

ED
Yes—

BUNNY
But I think there's something more basic here. Why
do you want to give me the garbage when you hate
it so much?

ED
I'm not giving it—

BUNNY
I just don't like the idea of having it thrust into my hands.

ED
I'm not thrusting.

BUNNY
You are thrusting.

ED
Why do you use these masculine images? I'm not thrusting, I'm trying to . . . *share* it with you! You have never had the freedom to take out the garbage before, and I want that experience for you!

BUNNY
Well. . . thank. . . you. . .

> *Silence. They turn front simultaneously, speak to us, confused, embarrassed, but still optimistic.*

Well it is a dilemma, of course, not that it can't be worked out, I have a great concern for the garbage, just as much as Ed does, because it seems to have this place of importance in our lives—

ED
Yeh, it serves as a kind of focal point for a lot of things, and if we could just focus on the focal point, things might come into better . . . focus.

BUNNY
Because in terms of taking responsibility, Ed has a tendency to give it all to me. And we thought perhaps we should work this out the way we work things out. Which we did. I stated that the garbage needs taking out.

ED
And I agreed. But I stated that I had a very negative response to her tone of voice in stating her statement.

BUNNY
So I tried a better tone of voice, in order to strike a balance between Ed's needs and those of the garbage. I tried a plain old "Take out the garbage."

ED
That's very blunt.

BUNNY
Ok. "Honey, I wonder if I might ask you to expel
the garbage?"

ED
It rings false.

BUNNY
Ok. *(more caricatured)* "Sweetheart, dearest, I know
you don't like to, because there's a lot on your mind
such as solving the world energy crisis and also paying the bills, but I really don't know where to put
any more garbage. Should I pile it in the bathroom,
or put it in the bed as a helpful hint, or serve it
again for dinner, or we could sleep in the garage and
use the house for the garbage but could you please
take it out?"

ED
I hate attempts at humor.

BUNNY
(broad caricature) "Oh, wook at this! It's the garbage! It would be so nice to do something with this!
But I need a big stwong man to do it! And evywone
will wook out their window and say, 'Wook at that
big stwong man going down those stairs! Doesn't he
take good care of her garbage!'"

ED
She really misses the whole point—

BUNNY
(belting it out) "Hey Ba-by, Haul My Garbage!"

> *Pause. She recovers demeanor.*

Uh, not to take away from our anniversary—

ED
No, because it is a very happy anniversary, really—

BUNNY
Really . . . really . . . incredible!

> *They turn to one another. After a moment
> they start to laugh.*

ED
Oh boy . . . I don't know how we got into all this—

BUNNY
Neither do I—

ED
I mean I don't think it's really a problem, it's just a new aspect of our relationship—

BUNNY
Though it is an aspect that's beginning to pile up.

He stops laughing.

ED
Look, I'm not trying to shove it under the rug—

BUNNY
No way, no way. Let's put it out in the *middle* of the rug. Some people have potted plants, we'll have canned fungus. The mold will just match the color scheme.

Silence. She waits.

Now you say something.

ED
(barely audible) No.

BUNNY
Don't repress it.

ED
I have to repress it.

BUNNY
You don't have to repress it.

ED
You're making me repress it.

BUNNY
I just said it: "Don't repress it, don't repress it."

ED
But your attitude is "Repress it, repress it."

BUNNY
All right then, repress it. Only repress it better!

ED

Now look, we both know that this has to come out
some way, and not destructively of course, but con-
structively so it brings us closer together—

BUNNY

Ok then do it do it do it do it!

ED

Ok. Ok I will! I am sick of it all, and it has nothing
to do with the garbage it's *(losing control)* YOU AND
THE JOB AND THE MARRIAGE I WANT TO THROW
UP I WANT TO BREAK EVERY WINDOW IN THIS
MOUSETRAP HOUSE I WANT TO GET IN THE CAR
AND DRIVE NINETY MILES AN HOUR TO CALIFOR-
NIA BECAUSE I CAN'T STAND THE THOUGHT OF
FIFTY MORE YEARS OF THE SAME DAMN THING I
WANT TO GIVE ALL THE WEDDING PRESENTS TO
GOODWILL AND YOU COME AT ME WITH THIS
MOUSY LITTLE SARCASTIC WHINE AND PATCH IT
UP WITH ONE SINCERE CONVERSATION A WEEK
AND WE MAKE A LIST THAT WE LOSE UNDER ALL
THE GARBAGE WE SPEW OUT NIGHT AND DAY AND
I'M SICK OF IT ALL!

Silence. After a long moment, he recovers.

Wow. I feel better.

BUNNY

(nearly inaudible) You do?

ED

Yes, I feel good. Do you feel good?

BUNNY

No.

ED

We have a better understanding.

BUNNY

Can I react to that?

ED

I don't need a reaction.

BUNNY

(contorted with rage) You ... INSENSITIVE ... IN-
SINCERE ... INSECURE ... IMMATURE—

Phone rings.

ED
Telephone.

> *She answers it. Total change of tone. Both*
> *react enthusiastically to the conversation.*

BUNNY
Hello? Oh Linda, hi! . . . Oh nothing. Just celebrat-
ing our anniversary. Talking things over, making
plans—

ED
Tell her about the house.

BUNNY
We looked at a new house. Oh it's incredible! Big
lawn, carpets, completely solar. . . George wants to
say Happy Anniversary.

ED
(taking phone) Hi. . . Yep, made it through the first.
Fifty more to go.

> *They laugh joyously.*

Oh yeh. Incredible. Everything is incredible. Ok.
Thanks for calling. Appreciate it. Bye.

> *He hangs up. Dead pause.*

BUNNY
Nice of them to call.

ED
We called them on theirs.

> *Long silence. They shift about, try to find*
> *some way to proceed, at last managing to*
> *speak the unspeakable:*

When do you want to see the lawyer?

BUNNY
I'll call Monday.

ED
You use ours. I'll find a new one.

BUNNY
Everything should be fifty-fifty.

ED
Even the garbage.

Silence.

BUNNY
It's good we can be mature about things.

ED
Make a rational judgment before we get . . . too involved.

BUNNY
You want me to pack you something?

ED
No, I'll stop by tomorrow.

Silence.

BUNNY
You know, I think we still are way, way ahead. A lot of couples, it takes, oh, six, seven years before they split. We've saved all those years.

Silence.

ED
I wonder what would happen if we . . . sort of. . .

BUNNY
Gave in? Compromised?

ED
Probably . . . set a bad precedent.

BUNNY
Yeh.

ED
(rising) Well, happy—

BUNNY
Yes, happy. . .

They start to shake hands. Freeze. Look at one another, amazed.

Incredible.

Blackout.

BON VOYAGE

Living room. Three chairs, facing front, as if toward TV. Millie, an ancient woman whose name we never know, enters, moves slowly to center chair. Feels to find seat, positions her posterior, lets herself drop into chair. Watches TV. Man enters.

BRAD
(calling off) Hon, you got a minute? Hi, Granny, what's on?

KARYN
(entering opposite) Hush, I just got the kids to sleep. What's on?

BRAD
(sitting) Karyn means what's on the TV, Granny?

KARYN
(sitting) Is she feeling all right?

BRAD
Oh, Granny's fine! Aren't you, Granny! She's just been a little funny ever since you left her sitting on the toilet for two hours.

KARYN
Well I'll help her start but I can't help her *do*.

BRAD
Wait. I got a surprise. Great news.

KARYN
You changed the furnace filter.

BRAD
I got my vacation dates.

KARYN
Vacation.

BRAD
First two weeks in July. Bon voyage.

KARYN
Bon voyage.

BRAD
Well, is that ok? Any problems?

KARYN
Fine. Where should we go?

BRAD
Usual place, I guess.

KARYN
I guess. Unless we want to venture out.

BRAD
It's hard to venture out in two weeks. You venture
out, then you venture right back in.

KARYN
Course the kids will go anywhere.

BRAD
With them, one place is as bad as another.

KARYN
And I'll go anywhere.

BRAD
The Poconos.

KARYN
Poconos.

BRAD
Granny likes the Poconos.

KARYN
And we like the Poconos.

BRAD
And the kids don't dislike the Poconos.

KARYN
There's a lot to be said for the Poconos.

BOTH
Bon voyage.

> *They sit, watching TV, brooding. Granny
> looks at one, then the other.*

BRAD
(in fantasy) Boy. If we weren't going to the Poconos,
I'd like to take a plane, fly the blue skies, go to a

place where it's sunny all day, lakes, people always happy, perfect harmony . . . Disney World!

KARYN
Wouldn't that be wonderful!

BRAD
(rising, overwhelmed) The perfect environment, an unspoiled dream! I mean see it now, before the developers move in. And what a thing for the kids! Everybody should make that pilgrimage just once in a lifetime!

KARYN
Really!

BRAD
The technology, the dream, the traditional values, the vision of the future, the fantastic financial success, how do they do that!

KARYN
Really wonderful!

BRAD
(slowly returning to reality) I mean sure it's expensive . . . and it's a long way for Granny . . . and Granny's chiropractor goes to the Poconos . . . so I guess . . . the Poconos.

He sinks back into his chair.

BOTH
Bon voyage. . .

They sit, watching TV, brooding. Granny discreetly clears her throat.

KARYN
(in fantasy) You know I shouldn't say it, but I've always had a dream that some day we'd just forget practical things, and we'd have this impulse, and we'd just up and go to . . . Paris, France!

BRAD
Wow!

KARYN
(rising, overwhelmed) Can you imagine? French restaurants! The Eiffel Tower!

BRAD
The Mona Lisa!

KARYN
Walk down the boulevards, run into Jackie Onassis!

BRAD
Cultural!

KARYN
Culture! Just imagine a place when you're speaking
English you're speaking a foreign language!

BRAD
The wine!

KARYN
The sewers of Paris!

BRAD
The real French fries!

KARYN
(slowly returning to reality)   If only it wasn't so far.
And Granny's bowel trouble. And Granny likes the
Poconos. So I guess . . . the Poconos. . .

>   *She sinks back into her chair.*

BOTH
Bon voyage. . .

>   *They sit, stewing. Granny sighs.*

BRAD
Disney World. . .

KARYN
Paris. . .

BRAD
If only it wasn't for—

KARYN
Sweetheart!

BRAD
(catching himself) Oh. No, I didn't mean—

KARYN
It's not Granny's fault!

BRAD
No. No, it's not!

>*They become frantically cheerful, clapping
her on the back until she wheezes.*

KARYN
She's not a burden!

BRAD
She's not a party pooper!

KARYN
She's not messing up our fondest dreams!

BRAD
We don't mind the sacrifice!

KARYN
As long as she's happy!

BRAD
We like the Poconos! We do! The kids—

KARYN
The kids go out and feed the mosquitoes! And that
wonderful museum of old farm equipment!

BRAD
Hike down the nature trails and teach your kids to
identify poison ivy, so when they grow up they can
hike down the nature trails and teach their kids to
identify poison ivy!

KARYN
And it should really be nice, because maybe by now
they've fixed the plumbing!

BRAD
Why sure, they're ready for Granny!

>*Silence.*

And us.

>*Silence.*

The Poconos.

BOTH
(muttering) Bon voyage.

Silence. They stew. Granny recovers.

KARYN
Well, what do you want to do tonight?

BRAD
Oh, keep Granny company, watch TV.

KARYN
Oh, there's a new commercial on. . .

GRANNY
You could go.

KARYN
(startled) What?

GRANNY
You could go.

BRAD
Go where?

GRANNY
On your vacation. Helen's not working. She could
look in on me.

KARYN
But she wouldn't.

GRANNY
She said she would.

BRAD
But you love the Poconos! We wouldn't be happy,
knowing you were here staring at the wall!

GRANNY
I hate the Poconos. Stare at the damn trees, while
the wind whistles up your tail.

They are stunned.

BRAD
She feels very strongly about it.

KARYN
She doesn't know what she's saying.

BRAD
Honey, we could. . .

KARYN
No we couldn't. . .

BOTH
(realizing) We could!

> *Both catapult from their chairs, circle*
> *about, not listening to one another.*

BRAD
Disney World! Wonderful! Mickey Mouse, the rides, Fantasy Land, Tomorrow Land, Cinderella's Castle. Oh honey, it's a dream come true!

KARYN
Our fondest dream, Paris, France, because Disney World, it's nice but it's unreal, but Paris! The kids can learn French, see the culture, the ruins, and the museums, all the art!

BRAD
Art! Mickey Mouse is art! Mickey Mouse is the highest form of American art! Give those kids pride in the best of our society today!

KARYN
And what a lesson in citizenship to be goodwill ambassadors, go to Paris and show the French that Americans are still the best!

> *Startled silence. Each at last realizes what*
> *the other has said. They come together in*
> *front of Granny, speaking simultaneously.*
> *She strains to see the TV.*

BRAD
Now wait a minute, you're talking about— We have to make reservations, because those reservations really fill up fast, because Disney World— What do you mean Paris? You mean Paris? Paris, France?

KARYN
(simultaneously) Are you still talking about Disney World? We have a chance to go to Paris. Right away before she changes— Get down there and make those reservations for Paris. What do I mean? Do I mean Paris? Well I don't mean Paris, Illinois!

> *They take a deep breath, resume.*

BRAD
What about the kids? Plastic is what they like.
Plastic is their identity. I will not alienate our chil-
dren from their plastic society!

KARYN
(simultaneously) I am thinking of the kids. These
children have grown up in a plastic society. They
don't know history, they don't know their roots!

They take a breath, continue murderously.

BRAD
All right forget the kids! *I* want to go to Disney
World! *I* want to go on the rides. I WANT TO SEE
MICKEY MOUUUUUSE!

KARYN
Paris is romance, and if you won't take me to Paris
you don't love me but I love you so I want a divorce.

BRAD
(raging) You want a divorce, you got a divorce. I
don't give a damn about you, oh no, but my job pays
for you and those kids and that television set—

KARYN
(simultaneously) You don't care for those kids, or
me. All you care about is your job and bank account
and checkbook and that damn television set—

BOTH
BON VOYAGE!

*They separate to opposite sides, frozen in
rage. At last, Granny sighs and breaks the
silence.*

GRANNY
I guess I would miss the Poconos. I think I'd like to
go to the Poconos.

BRAD
You . . . want to go . . . to the Po . . . conos?

GRANNY
The Poconos are calling me.

BRAD
(recovering) Oh . . . well sure . . . in that case. . .

KARYN
(recovering) We'd be happy to. . .

BRAD
Change our plans. . .

KARYN
I knew it was too good to last.

> *They look across at one another, brighten.*

BRAD
But we'll enjoy our vacation.

KARYN
Why of course, we always enjoy our vacation, and
some other time—

BRAD
Disney World, wouldn't it be wonderful!

KARYN
Wonderful, Disney World, or Paris!

> *Behind Granny, they embrace.*

BRAD
Paris, France! If only it wasn't for—

KARYN
(hushing him sharply) Po-conos!

BOTH
(mumbling) Bon . . . voyage. . .

GRANNY
I think I'm gonna buzz off now.

> *She snores, instantly asleep. They sit,*
> *sharing another bitter dream.*

BOTH
If only . . . it wasn't . . . for Granny. . .

> *Snore. Blackout.*

These are two-dimensional, cardboard characters. Having admitted that, we open the question of what that means. Sculpture, even the most realistic, eliminates the digestive organs, not to mention suntan, stutter and bank balance. In **Bon Voyage** and **Watchers**, the characters are likewise styled: they *are* their functions in the fable. In theoretical terms, character is a composite of drives encountering obstacles (or sometimes providing its own obstacles), with unique reactions, sometimes predictable, sometimes surprising, issuing from those encounters. In simpler terms, character is *whatever's necessary*.

Still, there's nothing artificial about these people. They must be as real as ourselves — our most stereotypical and two-dimensional selves. Actors' first instincts may be to play them *silly*, but *simple* is more accurate. They might be thought of, metaphorically, as amnesiacs. They can't remember quite how they got here, or who they're supposed to be; it only comes clear in fragments, then it's lost. They're simply caught in an exhausting maze of one-way streets, and when they do have a chance to make the proper turn, get straightened out and head back to Cincinnati, they miss it.

Perhaps because we feel so politically impotent, we place great value in *symbols*; this creates problems for artists dealing with ambivalent images. While some people feel, as we do, that Granny in **Bon Voyage** and **Watchers**, is the only sane, functional human being on stage, we've also heard, mainly from younger souls, "I was offended by your stereotype of the elderly," and "I don't feel she was typical of old people." We might respond that she's just one person, that Richard the Third and the Big Bad Wolf are not models of *all* kings or wolves, or that this whole impulse to see characters as "role models" is essentially Stalinist. To us, she's real: she's a San Quentin lifer who's very smart, but dumb when it's safer to be.

The characters in these sketches have the same names, or interchangeable ones. They might be the same people, or maybe not. They live in a world of Eds and Bunnys, Brads and Karyns, and they've forgotten why they're named that, though they each secretly sense that they're the most special Ed and Bunny in the neighborhood. Someday, they dream, people will know. And understand.

WATCHERS

Suburban den: Karyn reads newspaper.
Brad jogs in place. Granny, with thick
glasses, watches TV.

KARYN

Hon, what's the weather like?   It's supposed to snow.

BRAD

What if the car doesn't start?

KARYN

Well, we'd save on gas.

GRANNY

It's a blizzard out there.

KARYN

Granny, that's the TV.

GRANNY

TV's over there.

KARYN

No.

GRANNY

Well, I can't see.   These glasses, ever since I got these glasses I can't see.

BRAD

You can see.

GRANNY

I can't see.

BRAD

Look, we take care of you. We're responsible people. The doctor prescribed those glasses.   The doctor knows if you can see.

GRANNY

I couldn't see the doctor.

Distant scream.

BRAD
Is that the Johnsons?

KARYN
Wish they'd keep their window closed.

GRANNY
"Let's Make a Deal."

>   *Rises feebly, totters to window, squints, as*
>   *if viewing a TV screen.*

Oh no, it's one of those horrible violent things, I
wish they wouldn't show that stuff—

BRAD
She's worse than the kids.

KARYN
Well, she wants to go to a rest home.

BRAD
I'm not going to put my mother in a home. People
have to take responsibility.

KARYN
But she isn't happy here.

BRAD
She'll be happy whether she likes it or not.

GRANNY
(staring at window) I never seen the like, where
they got that woman, and what if there's children
saw that, what they're doing there—

BRAD
Granny, that is not the TV! That is a woman out in
the yard with— *(looking out window)* Omigod.

GRANNY
It's awful what they put on there.

BRAD
Honey.

KARYN
What?

BRAD
They've got that woman and they're— Omigod.

KARYN
(looking) Honey. . .

BRAD
Right in our neighborhood. Outside our window.
Quick. We can't let them get away with that.

KARYN
No.

BRAD
A lot of people stand around and let'em get away
with that, but we're not going to stand around and
let'em get away with that.

KARYN
We'll take responsibility.

BRAD
Responsibility. I know: we'll call the cops. Cause
the cops have got sophisticated computer communication and they'll be on the scene in seconds—

KARYN
(watching) Omigod. . .

BRAD
I'll do the dialing, you get the description. This is
the chance we've— No, you do the dialing. No, I'll
do the dialing. Won't the kids be proud!

> *Both are dialing the same phone. They
> continue in frantic, obsessively methodical
> action, accomplishing nothing. Screams.*

KARYN
Call the police.

BRAD
What's the number? I can't find the number.

KARYN
Find a pencil.

BRAD
Call the cops. C for cops. They can't get away with
this, crime, inflation, radiation—

KARYN
It's horrible—

BRAD
H for horrible—

KARYN
I can't find a pencil.

GRANNY
Is that the girl was on Johnny Carson? I thought
she was cute.

BRAD
Granny, that's the window!

GRANNY
Well I can't see! You're just a big white gob! My
only son is a big white gob!

BRAD
Those glasses are prescription glasses! Wait. We
have to take charge. Some people, they sit behind
their four walls and wait for the blizzard, but when
you got the chance to reach out and create positive
social change, it's gonna be here, not there, here!

GRANNY
I miss Arthur Godfrey.

BRAD
Look, dial Information. No, they charge for that—

KARYN
Our phone bill last month—

BRAD
(at phone) Get the description. I can't call the cops
without a description. How many are there?

KARYN
(at window) One, two, three, fo—

> *Scream, off.*

No, she doesn't count.

BRAD
Whatta they look like? You gotta know, cause when
they put you on the witness stand you have to be
precise or the defense attorney rips you to pieces.

KARYN
I can't find a pencil.

BRAD
One, two, three, and she doesn't count— But she
does count cause she's the human being, only we
gotta get a description—

KARYN
I can't find a pencil!

BRAD
(vehemently) Fix your hair!

KARYN
Why?

BRAD
You're gonna be a witness, you gotta look neat so
they believe you.

KARYN
I don't have anything to wear.

BRAD
(ready at phone) C'mon, whatta they look like?

KARYN
(looking) There's one black.

BRAD
Black? He must be underprivileged. *(toward window)* You underprivileged bastard!

KARYN
One with a leather jacket. He's white.

BRAD
White. He must be a young punk. You punk! One
black, one punk— What about the third guy? We
gotta see the third guy!

GRANNY
What's the commotion?

BRAD
SEE FOR YOURSELF!

GRANNY
I CAN'T SEE!

> *Sudden halt in the flurry. Faint screams.*
> *Ron becomes philosophical.*

BRAD

No. No. That's right. We're all blind to reality. We
do our jobs. We pay our bills. We feed our kids. We
ignore the writing on the wall.

GRANNY

I told'em not to scribble but you said the magic
marker would wash off and you're the daddy.

BRAD

We look in the papers. We look out for Number
One. We look through our rose-colored glasses right
into the teeth of the blizzard.

GRANNY

I could see better with my cataracts.

BRAD

(active again) Come on. The third guy, we gotta see
the third guy, cause we're not gonna stand around—
What about the third guy? There he is! He has absolutely *no* clothes on!

KARYN

They'll know him right away.

BRAD

That's no description. Look at his moles. They always have moles. Fix your hair.

KARYN

Find a pencil.

BRAD

Make a list.

KARYN

Look at his moles.

BRAD

Call the police. Police. *(rehearsing)* Ok. White,
black, no clothes, naked, leather jacket, girl. *(to
phone)* Operator, give me the police!

> *Karyn screams.*

What?

KARYN

It's starting to snow.

BRAD
(on phone) Police?

KARYN
She'll be in the snow. They'll leave her lying in the snow while we sit in here warm and comfortable, complaining about the gas bills, and she'll freeze in the snow. Where's the paper?

BRAD
Weather report. Find the paper.

KARYN
Fix your hair.

BRAD
Find a pencil.

KARYN
Make a list.

BRAD
Look at his moles.

KARYN
Call the police.

BRAD
(to phone) Police? *(to Karyn)* POLICE! IT'S THE PO- LICE! I CALLED THE POLICE! I REALLY CALLED THE POLICE! *(into phone)* OK, POLICE, HERE IT IS! YOU GET THIS! WHITE. BLACK. NO CLOTHES. NAKED. LEATHER JACKET. GIRL.

> *Hangs up.*

Thank God.

> *Total relief. He staggers into his wife's arms. They embrace.*

GRANNY
I'm going to see what else is on.

> *She sits, peers at the TV Guide.*

KARYN
Are you ok?

BRAD
Tired. I mean, there were three of'em.

KARYN
I'm so proud of you.

BRAD
Oh honey, for once in our life!

KARYN
But honey—

BRAD
Huh?

KARYN
It makes me think—

BRAD
No, it's good, it's really good—

KARYN
But . . . why is it . . . that we're more concerned . . .
about strangers . . . than about *us*?

BRAD
Oh no, it's *for* us. It's *for* us.

KARYN
All this . . . unbridled energy. When have we felt
this way . . . together?

BRAD
Oh, but honey—

KARYN
We've lost touch. I read the paper, you jog. We yell
at the kids, we clean up Granny. How long has it
been?

BRAD
(lyrically) Oh honey. I hear you calling to me. It's
like a sudden fanfare. What right do we have to
take responsibility for the whole world until we put
our own *selves* in order? It all begins at home. Oh
honey, let's not meddle in other people's lives. Let's
meddle in our own.

KARYN
Everything happens for a reason. It's a blessing in
disguise.

They kiss. Tableau.

GRANNY
I wish we could afford cable, you get a selection.

She rises, goes to window with TV Guide.

I don't miss nothing anyway, if they'd tone down some of the violence. Game shows are the worst. I could almost see better without these on. . .

She raises her glasses to forehead, peers out the window, slowly realizes.

There's a . . . dead woman . . . out there. . .

KARYN
The window's closed.

Long pause. Granny replaces her glasses, and again her world is a blur.

GRANNY
I wish they'd have more comedy.

Blackout.

Your coffee's poured, you glance at the paper
while the muffin toasts. You know the pop-up isn't
working right, but this time it will. Suddenly, smoke
rises and you're left with charcoal. **Doors** charts a
sudden veering out of control. We see it coming, but
we cling to our blind faith that the pop-up will somehow repair itself, that the magic dwarf down inside the
gizmo will wake up in time. Instead, we butter our ash
and eat it the rest of our lives.

For the actor, the challenge is to chart the stages
of the man's consuming rage to the point where the
dagger finally strikes home: when words are finally
said that stick to the skin like burning sugar. The father does love his daughter, he's intelligent, and up to
a point he's imaginative in trying to cope. The comedy
arises from those extravagant improvisations that
should work but don't. The tragedy is in the consequence: not simply that a child suffers pain that will
never be forgotten, but that a door is slammed shut
that stays shut forever.

Some technical notes: The door is the key image,
so it needs to have prominence. Ours was directly upstage. The act has also been played with an imaginary
door, the actors sitting on a chair faced upstage while
in the bathroom. The only trick is to avoid movement
that can be interpreted as toilet business. Furniture
and decor must be minimal, in order to represent credi-
bly two rooms thirty-five years apart with no change
whatever. Ours was nothing more than two chairs, a
table and a telephone.

How to make thirty-five years pass in a moment?
The simpler the better. A lighting cross-fade can help,
though not a blackout, but it has mostly to do with the
actor's internal change. The moment is prepared by
the father's own nausea at what he has just said. He's
suddenly very, very tired. He starts to rise, freezes in
startlement, holds in suspension as long as he possibly
can before his legs give out and he sinks into age like
plunging through a rotted ceiling. The startled freeze
is our genuine amazement that this could possibly be
happening to us.

What's Dad's name? When Joe Uher played him,
his name was Joe; when Conrad Bishop played him, it
was Conrad. Nobody calls him by name, and we never
know his name, but he knows.

DOORS

*Table with telephone. Chairs. A door.
Dad enters hurriedly from another direction, putting on jacket, checking keys. He
speaks to Kathy, a small girl, unseen behind the closed door.*

DAD
Kathy, come on, we've gotta pick up Mommy. How
much longer you gonna be?

KATHY
(off) Ok, Daddy.

DAD
You need any help in there?

KATHY
I'm ok, Daddy.

DAD
Kathy, would you hurry and finish? I need to use
the bathroom too before we go. *(tying his shoe, to
himself)* Just once I would like to answer the call of
nature at the time it is issued. *(to her)* Come on,
hon, Mommy's waiting. I'm not asking for a world
record, just a good sporting effort. Open the door.

KATHY
I can't.

DAD
Honey, don't play games.

KATHY
It's got a lock on it.

He stops.

DAD
Did you lock the door? Ok, just turn the little lock
thing and come out.

KATHY
It's locked.

DAD
Kathy, why did you do that?

KATHY
Brian did it.

DAD
Brian is with Mommy. Kathy, we told you not to
lock this door. *(trying to open door)* How many
times did we tell you never to lock the door?

KATHY
I wanna be private.

DAD
This is ridiculous. Open the door.

KATHY
Daddy, you lock it sometimes. You won't let me in
the bathroom when *you* go potty.

DAD
(slowly, distinctly) Honey, I'll tell you how to open
the door. Listen to Daddy. Now you see the knob.
Now you see the little lock thing inside there?

KATHY
Daddy, my shoe's untied.

DAD
(losing patience) Kathy, Mommy's waiting, we don't
have time—

KATHY
I want Mommy to do it.

DAD
Mommy's downtown!

> *Strangled sound from bathroom.*

Kathy?

> *Another. Panicked:*

Are you all right?

> *He pulls desperately to open door.*

What have you got in your mouth!

KATHY
Vuh towel!

She laughs. He recovers, suppressing rage.

DAD
I am going to count to five. One. Two. Three—

KATHY
All right.

DAD
Come on out.

KATHY
I can't.

DAD
One. Two. Three—

KATHY
I'm coming!

DAD
Then do!

KATHY
Unlock the door!

He controls himself. She snivels.

DAD
Ok. Honey. Now listen. Calm down. Daddy's here.

KATHY
Daddy, are there any bugs in the bathroom?

DAD
There are no more bugs. Daddy killed all the bugs.

KATHY
I don't like bugs.

DAD
Neither does Daddy. Now take hold of the handle—

KATHY
It's a doorknob.

DAD
Doorknob. Now turn it to your right. You know
your right hand? The side you eat with your spoon.

KATHY
I'm hungry, Daddy.

DAD
Now turn it to your right.

KATHY
When I come out, can I have some cereal?

DAD
Yes you can. Now are you turning it?

KATHY
Can I have Captain Crunch?

DAD
If we have any, if Mommy bought any—

KATHY
I think she did.

DAD
No she didn't—

KATHY
In Captain Crunch you get a secret message writer.

DAD
Now turn it toward the wall!

KATHY
Now which wall do you mean now, Daddy?

DAD
The right wall!

KATHY
Is that my spoon hand?

DAD
Yes!

KATHY
Is this the hand?

DAD
I can't see through the door!

KATHY
(shrieking) Daddy!

DAD
(aghast) What!

KATHY
What makes the toilet flush?

DAD
COME OUT OF THERE THIS MINUTE!

> *Phone rings. He dithers, then rushes to answer it.*

Hello! . . . Yes, I am trying to pick you up, I have a slight problem. Kathy is locked in the bathroom. Well, she did. I *know* I should have fixed the damn door but I didn't!

KATHY
Daddy—

DAD
Kathy, be quiet, Mommy's on the phone—

KATHY
I wanta talk to Mommy!

DAD
(on phone) Hold on, I'm trying to explain.

> *Begins methodically, becoming more and more incomprehensible, pacing about, gesturing with the receiver.*

Kathy, ok, now listen, I'll tell you how to get out. Now you put your thumb and index finger on it and push down on the side near the wall at the same time you're pushing up on the side near the bathtub. Now turn the doorknob counterclockwise. You know which way the clock goes? Ok, the big hand is at the top, it falls down to the right and it zoops up the other side, that's clockwise, and counterclockwise means against clockwise— *(furiously, to phone)* THEN WHAT DO YOU SUGGEST?

> *Listens. Again calm:*

Kathy, Mommy has a suggestion. Mommy says pretend it's a book, you're turning the page of a book.

KATHY
What book?

DAD
Any book.

KATHY
I want CAT IN THE HAT.

DAD
CAT IN THE HAT—

KATHY
You read it.

DAD
We're not going to read it, that's not the point!

KATHY
(wailing) I want a story!

DAD
Mommy has another suggestion! *(listening)* She
says. . . Pretend that you're taking a pinch of fairy
dust— *(to phone, exasperated)* Oh come *on*! Look,
can't you take the bus? Kathy, so help me I'm going
to spank you so hard you can't sit down for a month!

She wails. He yells into phone.

No! I won't! I won't! Just get off the phone!

*He hangs up. Kathy wails. He tries to
light a cigarette, shreds it, utterly frazzled.*

Kathy, are you a little girl or are you a big girl? If
you're a little baby, then that's exactly the way
we're gonna treat you. Open the door.

KATHY
(wailing) I can't!

DAD
Stop whining! *(mimicking)* "I ca-a-a-an't!"

KATHY
(wailing) Don't *do* that!

DAD
(mimicking) "Don't do-o-o-o-o that!"

KATHY
(wailing) No-o-o-o-o!

DAD
I'm not going to listen to that, Kathy. I'm going to
pick up Mommy.

KATHY
(terrified) Don't go away!

DAD

I *will* go away, and it's going to get dark, and you'll
be all alone in the dark!

KATHY

No-o-o-o-o-o!

DAD

Honey, we'll have your favorite food for dinner tonight—

KATHY

I don't want any dinner!

DAD

Stop crying! You are totally repulsive when you do
that. *(grasping at the last strand)* Kathy, you better
come out because there might be some bugs in
there. Daddy doesn't know if he got all the bugs.

KATHY

(beside herself) Don't want any bugs!

DAD

Well there might be some bugs!

> *Totally possessed with rage, he picks up a
> chair, rushes at the door. Stops abruptly,
> puts the chair down, tries to regain control.*

Kathy, I am calm. And I want you to be calm. Now
this is a family, and if you don't learn to share you'll
be a very unhappy person, and you don't want me to
tell Mommy *(with increasing vehemence)* what a little
baby you are, cause that's what she's going to think,
she's going to think you're just a whining, selfish,
stupid stupid stupid little baby, that's what Mommy's going to think, and she won't even come home,
she'll take Brian and leave you to be the WHINY, RE-
PULSIVE LITTLE LUMP OF LARD AND THAT'S
EXACTLY WHAT YOU DESERVE!

> *He stops, appalled, sinks into a chair.
> Dead silence. Kathy's voice is very small.*

KATHY

Daddy?

DAD

What?

KATHY
I know a joke.

DAD
What?

KATHY
When I get big, and you get old, they take you and
cut stuff out.

> *She giggles. He exhales heavily, starts to
> rise, half-turning. Freeze. He sinks back
> into the chair.*
>
> *Thirty-five years pass instantly. Next mo-
> ment, the door opens and Kathy emerges.
> She is now a mature woman, harried and
> brusque. He is an old man, recovering
> from surgery.*

I was in there. What do you want?

DAD
Help me up.

KATHY
What for?

DAD
Bathroom.

KATHY
You left your robe. Let me bring you the pan.

DAD
Help me up.

> *She helps him walk slowly to the door.*

KATHY
Dad, this is a serious operation for a person your
age, and if you always have to haul up and stagger
to the bathroom—

DAD
I want to be private.

KATHY
You can't go alone.

DAD
Shut the door.

KATHY
You can't put yourself on the pot!

> *He goes in, closes door. She paces, nervous-*
> *ly searching for a cigarette.*

All right. Fall, break a hip, your other kid won't
help. Are you ok in there?

DAD
(off) Yes.

KATHY
Did you lock the door?

DAD
I want to be private.

KATHY
I think there's something wrong with you. So does
Brian, only he won't say straight out.

DAD
Where's the paper?

KATHY
It's right beside you on the left hand wall. What are
you gonna do if you can't get the door open?

> *Phone rings. She answers.*

Yes? Yeh, he's in the bathroom. Locked himself in.
Can't even find the toilet paper.

DAD
I found it.

KATHY
I'm on the phone! *(to phone)* He stays in there, I
have to go pick up the kids. No, I don't want to put
him in a home, but I sure am thinking about it.

DAD
Who is it?

KATHY
I'm on the phone! Are you a baby? If you're a baby,
then that's how we're gonna treat you! *(to phone)*
Sure, I'm the dumb one. I just hope I never live that
long. That's too long for any person to live. Two
kids and an old man who thinks he's a grownup.

> *She looks up, sees him standing in the doorway, staring at her.*

I have to hang up.

> *Hangs up.*

Brian says hello.

DAD
Yeh.

KATHY
Tired?

DAD
Ok.

> *She goes to him, helps him to chair.*

KATHY
Hold on.

DAD
Easy.

KATHY
Ok?

DAD
Hurts.

> *He sits in the chair. She straightens his collar, smiles, straining to be jocular.*

KATHY
Any bugs in there?

> *Silence.*

That was a joke.

DAD
No jokes.

KATHY
I'll be home about four.

> *She picks up purse, hurries out. Alone:*

DAD
No jokes.

> *Fade.*

Part Three
GETTING OURS

It's the little things that count. Most of us look World Hunger in the eye courageously: it takes more than a few million starving Ethiopes to make us blink. But try to swat a fly with a plastic-handled swatter. Has the Judeo-Christian tradition come to this: trillions to kill Reds, but a swatter whose handle snaps? Sure, this weapon is only a bargaining chip, but this fly has no incentive to negotiate: he'll buzz his little butt through millennia.

The four acts that follow are about the maddening buzz of desire and our brittle flailing to swat it. We seem to regard our own reality as a jail from which we fantasize escape through an indiscriminate granola mix of needs, both urgent and absurd. In leisure time, we pay to slip away from pinpricks of daily life into chainsaw massacres created by special effects crews. We hire others to dream for us, while our own dream life nurses only vague images of the prize ticket, or of some major cataclysm that might get us a day off work.

But if these characters find inadequate escape, we hope they offer, for the audience, an escape not *from* reality but *into* reality. We might try walking through a locked door by painting the door in bright pastels, but it'll really work better to turn a key in the lock. Tacky reality may be our jail, but it's also our key. There's an amazing spirit in high school basketball that's utterly lacking in the TV pros. Ballet is unforgettable from the first row: the dancers' sweat, the slippers' squeak, the gravity fighting that awesome urge to flight. And the street clown's backflip is as amazing as if Aunt Helen did it. Extraordinary energy flows from stroking that bumpy, dry skin of Reality — the streets of Cleveland aren't the Yellow Brick Road, but the dusty feet are the same.

With dusty feet, a baby on the way and no money in the bank, we created the first sketch, **Dreamers**, in 1974. Since then, we've played it over a thousand times — remarkable span for a playlet with no setting, no characters, no story and precious little meaning. What does a mirror *mean*?

Yet audiences respond. For years, **Dreamers** was our show opener — a barometer to predict what each audience would laugh at. Some funny lines, yes, but surprising responses simply to the act of *naming* wants, to the rampant scramble through a potluck of casseroles, baked beans, and Jello Supremes in battered cake pans without touching a bit of sustenance. The sketch does have a vague action: the characters go from raw desire to encounters with flat denials, then masked denials, self-denials, and at last, bald proclamations of Contentment. But that's secondary to the fact that they just sit there, stand, move and *want*.

Recently, **Dreamers** went through new incarnation as an experimental video for Philadelphia public television. Taped during all-night sessions in the first level of Philadelphia's three-block downtown Gallery shopping mall, we found ourselves among the midnight cleaning crews, security guards, unidentified passersby and blocks of cluttered emptiness. The characters peered through gratings at the captive merchandise, waded through frozen reflecting pools, walked in the darkened arteries of their dreams, trudged up the down escalator.

Technically, it was a tough acting job: trying to change the context and *dis*-remember lines we'd said, rapid-fire, for a thousand shows. But we also discovered the extraordinary power of a dramatic piece, even one that's not of Shakespearean stature, to be a focusing lens and reveal new facts about itself after years and years of squeezing dry. The endless retakes due to ambient noise were like a reprise of the hundreds of showings of the piece itself. And we realized that its meaning was tied to the fact that these characters have said each of these lines dozens, thousands of times, and the retakes go on till their tape runs out.

The performers need to trust its simplicity without working to make it funny. Age transitions should be suggested but not emphasized. We performed the sketch speaking directly to the audience in a rapid, conversational tone, initially sitting in two chairs faced front, then winding up the same. The trick is to put contradictions in tight juxtaposition, to let the audience catch things in passing. And to keep in mind that whatever it is we want, it's not exactly what we say. We're sitting there telling the audience a forthright, pleasant, engaging, enormous lie.

DREAMERS

Man and woman sit, facing front. They speak rapidly, intensely, transforming through a lifetime of faces.

JES
Want.
Wish.
Wish for.
Crave.
Need.
Desire.
Require. . .

STU
Prefer.
Have an eye to.
Have a mind to.
Set the heart on.
Covet.
Hanker for.
Long for.
Pine for.
Hope for. . .

JES
Sigh for.
Lust after.
Yearn for.
Hunger for.
Want.

Freeze. Shift.

I want just the basics: food, shelter, love.

STU
I want a dog.

JES
I want just one kind word.

STU
I want a baseball glove.

JES
I want something to stop the pain.

STU
I want a little appreciation.

JES
I want an ice cream cone.

STU
I want the car Friday night.

JES
I want your solemn word.

STU
I want everything I can get.

JES
I want to get out of this town.

STU
I want to speak French.

JES
I want a bicycle with gears.

STU
I want recognition.

JES
I want to try biofeedback.

STU
I want a real relationship.

JES
I want to be alone.

STU
I want to go to California.

JES
I want to be a movie star.

STU
I want to make a lot of money.

JES
I want to get well.

STU
I want peace.

JES
I want a total reordering of society.

STU
I want to forget all about it.

JES
I want out.

STU
I want in.

JES
I want food for my baby.

STU
I want a decent job.

JES
I want her to die.

STU
I want to get even.

JES
I want to have a lot of friends.

STU
I want to show 'em what jerks they are.

JES
I want a Barbie doll.

STU
I want to join the Cub Scouts.

JES
I want a letter from home.

STU
I want to be an architect.

JES
I want to see my grandchildren.

STU
I want to find out what it's like.

JES
I want the basic things.

Sudden rush of hunger:

STU

I want a coke and combat boots and I want to go fishing and have a great time and I want to see the world and meet all kinds of people and I want to have a good marriage and two wonderful kids and I want a divorce and I want some peace and quiet and some teeth that fit and I want a glass of water and a Digital Action Racecar Set.

JES

I want a dolly that wets and talks about it and you can curl her hair and even buy her a boyfriend and I want to stop hearing about one toy after another and stop picking up after everyone I want some household help. And I want to get my bowels in order and stop worrying could it be a tumor. I want to go to school and draw pictures and I want a picture of everything so I know how everything looks.

Freeze. Shift.

STU

I want to play with the typewriter.

JES

No, you'll break it.

STU

I want to control my own life.

JES

You have responsibilities.

STU

I want to write a novel.

JES

You don't have the time.

STU

I want to find the time.

JES

You don't have the talent.

Freeze.

I want to be totally weird.

STU

You have responsibilities.

JES
I want a candy bar.

STU
You already had a candy bar.

JES
I want to feel the elephant.

STU
You might get stepped on.

JES
I'd like some Oriental food.

STU
Well, there's a McDonald's.

Freeze.

I want to have my ashes scattered.

JES
No, it's against the law.

STU
I want to try what I read about.

JES
No, it's against the law.

STU
I want to leave my parents.

JES
No, it's against the law.

STU
I want to say what I feel.

JES
No, it's against the law.

STU
I want to break the law.

JES
No.

Freeze. They shift into realistic interplay.

I want to have another baby.

STU

Oh. Well I feel exactly the same way, honey. Sure.
It's just going to be necessary to find a good time
when we can sit down and talk and figure what bud-
get we have and when might be the best time and
then we can plan when we might have another baby
without having all the problems that might come up
which I think we can avoid if we just find a good
time when we can sit down and talk.

Silence. Suddenly he leaps up as a child.

I wanna play in the mud!

JES

(holding him by wrist) Well it's fine to play in the
mud as long as you remember—

STU

Yeh Momma—

JES

That you have to be careful and remember that
Momma works hard to keep you looking your best
and Momma would be upset if she found you playing in the mud and you hadn't remembered and forgot that it's ok to play in the mud as long as you
keep clean.

Freeze. Shift. They are alone, bitter.

STU

I want to get something nice for my wife . . . but
she'd rather I saved the money. I want to do something really big . . . but I have to consider my family.
I want to stop smoking but I know I won't.

JES

I want to see my grandchildren . . . but I like my
privacy. I want to pray . . . but I'd be laughed at. I
want to stay young . . . but I'd better act my age.

STU

I want to hit that sonofabitch, but he'd hit me back.
I want to scream, but people would turn around.

JES

I want to scream, but people would turn around. I
want to pray, but I'd be laughed at.

STU
I want to do all kinds of things, but I'm too young.

JES
I want to do all kinds of things, but it's too late.

STU
I want to raise white rats, but I have to consider my family.

> *Long silence. Suddenly jovial, they rise, embracing.*

JES
I want it. But I don't need it.

STU
I want it. But not as much.

JES
That's all I want.

STU
I'm satisfied.

JES
I'm really full.

STU
That's enough.

JES
I don't want another thing.

STU
The horn of plenty.

JES
Everything I could ever want.

STU
My heart's content.

JES
What else could I want?

STU
I'm content.

JES
Well-provided.

STU
Cup runneth over.

JES
I've had enough.

STU
I've had more than enough.

JES
I've . . . had it.

Their smiles freeze, decay. Blackout.

THE ENTREPRENEUR

Bank office. Woman sits at desk: a Vice President. Man appears, wearing zipper jacket and baseball cap. He stands till he's noticed. Smiles, waves.

MS. BOTKIN
Hello. What can I do for you?

JERRY
You're a Vice President. You must be pretty smart to be a woman Vice President. It's not every day you meet a woman Vice President.

MS. BOTKIN
Well thank you.

JERRY
(sitting in chair) Ok. Down to business. My name's Jerry, and well, as to work, I've done a lotta different kinds, I drove a taxi, wow, that's something, and I pumped gas, all kinds of things where I got a lotta experience—

MS. BOTKIN
You're looking for a loan.

JERRY
(surprised) Right. That's exactly right. I spose you could tell when I walked in here, I bet.

MS. BOTKIN
People often come here for that reason.

JERRY
Well, you're right. See, I thought: WHAT AM I DO-ING? My dad, he was a maintenance man, keeping things in good maintenance, and he used to say, "Jerry, look, if you wanna be rich, this is a free country, it's up to you." He was never rich, but that's cause he had a lotta work to do. But he told me, he said, "You wanna be rich, just make up your mind to do it." So I did.

MS. BOTKIN
You did what?

JERRY
I wanna be rich.

MS. BOTKIN
I see.

JERRY
Well I mean I wanna get a loan and start my own
business.

MS. BOTKIN
Oh. Well. What is it you had in mind to do?

JERRY
A steel mill.

MS. BOTKIN
A steel mill?

JERRY
Oh I know a lot of people start small, like a McDonald's franchise or a barbershop, but I thought why
start small, cause you kinda defeat yourself before
you start. So I thought how about a steel mill,
cause there's always a need for steel, and I know
they talk about oil and petroleum, but I thought if I
make it in steel then I could do oil as a sideline.

MS. BOTKIN
Well, Mr. . . . Jerry—

JERRY
I know. I know what you're going to say: What
makes you think you could run a steel mill? Right?

MS. BOTKIN
That did cross my mind.

JERRY
That doesn't matter. I don't need to know. I can
hire guys that already know. You know how many
guys are outa work now? See, we're in an Economic
Boom right now, boom, all these places going boom,
boom, all these guys outa work. So I just put an ad
in the paper, I get all I need. See, it's just a matter
of somebody having the idea to do it. That's Free
Enterprise.

MS. BOTKIN
Jerry. . . Do you have any business experience?

JERRY

Experience! Listen! Experience, right? Listen!

Pregnant pause.

I used to run the elevator at the Sears Building.

MS. BOTKIN

(at a loss) Did you.

JERRY

You know. All these executives, every day, up and down, up and down, and they don't even think about the elevator operator, they don't know you exist, you're not nothing, you're a piece of gum on the floor. So they talk to each other, up and down, up and down, and I'm listening, up and down. You know something? In that time I would say that I got the equivalent of a College Education.

MS. BOTKIN

I meant more in the area of—

JERRY

No, I catch your drift. I get it. You gotta take precautions that I'm not some bum off the street, right? That if you loan me a loan it's gonna pay off, right? Cause you're a Vice President, that's your job.

MS. BOTKIN

Yes it is.

JERRY

Well, to level with you frankly, I would have to say no. Strictly speaking. But I know a sure-fire idea when I think of it. Like the Lottery: if there's that many losers, then there's gotta be a winner. See, here's my idea... I can trust you, can't I?

MS. BOTKIN

I'm sure you can.

JERRY

Ok. The key to the whole thing is get a monopoly. Say if you got Park Place and I got Boardwalk, it doesn't do us any good, because we can't even build houses on it, let alone hotels. But see, if I get'em both, then wow, I mean there's nothing you can do cause you're gonna land there sooner or later. Wow! That's my idea.

MS. BOTKIN
Yes, well—

JERRY
See it kinda has—

MS. BOTKIN
The virtue of simplicity.

JERRY
Yeh.

MS. BOTKIN
Jerry—

JERRY
I know. I know what you think. See, that's one at-
tribute of mine, I can tell what people think. You
think: SO WHAT? Right? Ok, here's the trick.

Leans in, with great deliberation:

There's all these big steel mills, right? They think
they got it made. They think, "Ho ho, I got this
business tied up so tight, nobody could just come
along and start a steel mill!" So they're not gonna
be watching me. They'd probably even laugh at me.
They'd go HO HO. So while they're sitting up there
smoking big cigars, here I am getting set, I'm cogi-
tating and I'm making a list. Like maybe I'll have
my factory out in the country where nobody's even
gonna notice. And then just when they think HO
HO, and they take a puff and they let down their
guard, then all of a sudden SHAZAM! BOARDWALK!
BAM! PARK PLACE! And there it is.

Silence. She tries to find words.

MS. BOTKIN
Jerry. I have really enjoyed talking to you, but I
have some other work, and I think you have a lot of
good ideas, but . . . it isn't really practical. There is
no way you could start a steel mill. You have to be a
different kind of person to do things like that. Not a
matter of a better person or a worse person, just a
different person. If it was just a matter of making
up your mind, I'm sure a lot more people would have
done it. I myself. . . I don't really make that much
money, surprising as it may seem. So I'm afraid—

JERRY

See, I talked to you cause I thought, here she is, she's a woman, she's probably liberated. I mean like New Ideas, I mean like Progress, I mean ZAPPO! VICE PRESIDENT! LIBERATED!

Silence. Cheerful again:

No that's ok. I know. Just promise me you won't use my idea. Ok?

MS. BOTKIN

Don't worry.

JERRY

Listen, can you do me a favor?

MS. BOTKIN

I'm not sure—

JERRY

It's just I gotta make a very important business telephone call, and I don't have a quarter. Could I use your phone? It's local. I won't monopolize the telephone waves.

MS. BOTKIN

All right.

He picks up receiver, pokes push buttons. Delighted:

JERRY

Dad? It's Jerry. Know where I'm calling from? Vice President of the bank, right in the office. Yeh! Listen, I talked to'em about this deal, see, and they're not saying yes right away, cause money's tight and they gotta check things out. But mainly I made this great contact. This woman is a Vice President, so you know she's gotta be smart, and she asked some very pertinent questions. I just wanted to let you know. Yeh, dinner on Sunday. Bye.

Hangs up. Giggles. Goes to door.

Thanks. Hey now, remember: Boardwalk! Park Place! Bam! Shazam!

Blackout.

The preceding act, **Entrepreneur**, is about success; the next, about hard cash. Both were created for our 1975 revue **THE MONEY SHOW.**

Years ago at a San Francisco theatre, we saw a sketch about a taxi driver applying for an office job as professional Smiler. This became the inspiration for our Entrepreneur. The "steel mill" premise came from joking riffs about prospects of Milwaukee mom & pop taverns going multinational: Harry & Edna's National Bank. Oddly, it wasn't until we'd played this sketch successfully for years, then by chance saw it performed by an inexperienced but gifted Drexel University freshman, that we saw the character's *reality*. He brought to it a madly consuming, desperate faith that lifted it, at long last, beyond the stage image we'd begun with. To this man, *rich* is a very special state of validation and empowerment. At the end, his hope is plucked out, but because it's only hope, it can easily grow back.

Nina, Ray & Earl is based on real models. Its theme is so blindingly simple that it might easily be missed. In every speech, at every stage of the people's lives, money has the grim dynamic force of a Greek god. The bare terror of the need is so much a part of them that they have no sense of the degree to which it's warped their emotional lives. Sex is a wealth symbol, not vice versa. The dollar is a vampire invited to the cocktail party; he's a smashing success, but your party gets a little strange by midnight.

The act draws also on the loneliness of sitting for a portrait. Suddenly your soul drains from your face and puddles in your toes. The notion of being *seen* should be universally pleasurable, and most of us seek it avidly. Yet most of us can tolerate it only in small doses, even from our beloveds. So this trio, forced by the stage to explain themselves, are like all portraits: images of isolation.

Despite the bleak frame, we would hope these portraits have a faint spark of the same humanity as the dozens of Rembrandts before which we've stood amazed. Too often we look at others to see if we should hire'em, seduce'em, ignore'em or report'em. There can be great pleasure just in looking to *see*: to rediscover the human race simply by looking at it. Even the most exceptionally ugly nose can make us all the more conscious and treasuring of the noses we hold dear.

NINA, RAY & EARL

Three figures, facing front, in separate chairs. They sit, stand, turn, move about, going nowhere.

NINA

High school boys are such creeps. They buy you a hamburger they wanta feel you above. If they add a malt it's below.

RAY

You work after school for a few bucks a week, then you take'em out, they want you to feed'em, entertain'em. Then they give you one goodnight smack.

EARL

The old man pounds it in my head, "Work hard, save your money." I decided Bullshit. If I got it I'll spend it. I got a piece of every little tail in town.

NINA

My mother said, "Congratulations, you're graduated, get a job."

RAY

I go two years to college, my dad says, "What have you learned that's worth what I'm paying?"

EARL

Not worth it.

RAY

So I quit.

EARL

I graduated. Major in agriculture. And it's the Depression.

RAY

Right into the army.

EARL

And it's pure accident this girl, her old man's in the clothing business, and she proposes to me. She's bringing in the money, so she proposes to me.

NINA

I work and see how these bozos are. I'd never marry
somebody way above me in terms of money, they
think they paid for you and you're the chicken in the
pot. I got a guy that's not afraid of work. Machin-
ist. We just make ends meet.

RAY

Four years in the army.

EARL

So I accept.

RAY

Blind alley.

EARL

Mistake number one.

NINA

One daughter. There was a son, I just had the feeling he coulda lived if the doctor'd known what to do.
Richard. We still had to pay the bill. But there's
one daughter.

EARL

Thinks she owns me.

RAY

They like you on payday.

EARL

I says, "You don't own me!"

RAY

They don't look you in the face.

EARL

So I drink.

NINA

I says it's dangerous on those machines. He says
sure but that's his job, there's gotta be a job. It took
his arm right off. And he only left bills to pay.

RAY

Then I got married.

EARL

She divorced me.

RAY

Had to knuckle down.

EARL

Live it up.

RAY

Then I get into this Chevy agency. I got like they say a kind of natural gift of selling. They gotta like you. It ain't always easy, say some good-for-nothing or a dago, say, you hafta smile, treat'em like a big shot. So I get in the money. Then I run into Nina.

EARL

Married twice and the same both times. Money. I make it, throw it away, they can't stand that. They want you to spend it on'em, then you get married they want you to save it. Make up your mind. I lived in forty-two states. Then I run into Nina.

NINA

I run into a brick wall. Try to get welfare, they tell you quit your job, can't help you if you're working. Imagine that? So I worked. Had to support my girl. File clerk. How long's it been, eighteen years? Jeez. I thought if I get married again, how'm I gonna know the man's ok, maybe he won't support us. So I stayed single. I met Ray. He's got two kids, don't get along with his wife. We have some good times. He brings down a load of groceries every week.

RAY

I'd walk in with two big bags of groceries, and those eyes'd just light up.

NINA

He said he wanted to marry me.

RAY

But hell, here I'd be paying child support, alimony. There's no way.

NINA

I'd never have a man supporting some other woman.

RAY

That's why I bought the dealership, I thought I'll make a mint of money, I'll get the damn divorce. Mint of money.

NINA
A husband supports his wife.

RAY
She didn't complain when I brought the groceries.

EARL
She was going with this other guy, and here I come
into the picture.

NINA
Ray's ok, but then Earl, Earl likes a good time, and I
like a good time—

EARL
We got a lot in common—

NINA
But there's not that much in common.

RAY
I says, "I know you been stepping out. After all I
done for you!" The dealership, see, I thought it'll get
better. Cause I can sell cars. People have got to
have cars. And I borrowed too much, did a couple of
things, they— So I go out in the garage— It wasn't
on her account, it's on account of the bank— And I
take a hose, siphon hose, and. . .

He tries to explain, can't find words, quits.

NINA
It was the bank and all the debts.

EARL
I'd never done that. I'd have a few drinks.

NINA
There's still Earl—

EARL
You got old Earl—

NINA
But at my age you got to think of more than good
times. Friend of mine, she marries this old guy, he
sits around the house, wears out the springs on her
sofa. She goes out scrubbing floors.

EARL
We got each other.

NINA

So what we got? No. No, I don't think so. My
daughter's grown, I'll have my pension, social security. The house is paid off. I'm set up pretty good.

EARL

Whine about money. She says, "Whatcha do if you
get sick, you don't even have insurance." I tell her,
"I don't have insurance for being alone." What
about that? What about being alone?

NINA

Not so bad. It's really not. It's not bad.

Waits.

It's not really bad. Being alone. It's not bad.

RAY

It cost fifteen hundred to put me in a hole. Besides
the flowers. Christ. I coulda used the dough.

Blackout.

Monopoly was first written for **THE MONEY SHOW**, a revue produced in Chicago to a remarkable lack of acclaim as we were coping with a foul basement apartment, a newborn child, a troublesome pancreatic tumor (which, like the child, proved benign) and no ready cash. It was revised for a revue at University of Delaware, played with fierce intensity by the student cast, and incited a pained phone call from the department chairman the day after opening: loved the show, hated **Monopoly**. Violent. Offensive. Inappropriate for students.

Of course the same might be said of **HAMLET**. To be sure, **Monopoly** is a nasty little piece with no poetry in its soul to mitigate the atrocities. But the man didn't know his students. In fact, they brought to it a harsh awareness of the characters' arrested development — souls in their mid-thirties who still wait for the test score. Who are still confused undergraduates in their secret hearts. Who wake daily to the bleak terror of the sagging and the balding. Who can't recall whether it's Tuesday or Wednesday, because it really makes little difference.

Still, our Delaware contretemps carries a lesson about revues. Including work that violates the general tone that the audience is led to expect by the first couple of pieces in the show is a bit like showing slides of crippled children to people who thought they were invited to a beer party. We like to take that risk, but unity of tone is rarely violated with impunity: your guests may not come back. The joy of a revue is that it *can* be so kaleidoscopic, but the audience must be bundled up in warm mufflers and strapped in tightly to get ready for the wild ride.

We make no claim that staging the tribulations of the human race gives Fast Pain Relief. The popular objections these days to just about anything serious: "That's depressing." "We already know that. We see it on the news every day." "I don't want to see frustration and famine and murder and rape. I get plenty of that at home." But theatre is a *public trial* of these acts, and if we're all convicted, then we might stand some chance at forgiveness. Absurdity loves company, and none of us has arrived at so-called maturity without, at some one time, behaving as absurdly, as hysterically, as destructively as these characters do. If we share nothing else, we share this.

MONOPOLY

*Four people, all in their mid-thirties, sit
around the table, playing Monopoly and
drinking wine: Teresa, a beautiful, taste-
fully dressed editor; Walter, her compan-
ion, a large, hearty real estate developer
who always looks rumpled no matter how
well he dresses; Austin, a slight, dapper
academic in wire-rimmed glasses; and
Alice, Austin's wife, an ex-painter whose
life has gone drab.*

*Walter rolls dice and moves his piece. An
exclamation from the group:*

TERESA
Boardwalk! How lucky can you get!

WALTER
Hey, hey, I'll buy it!

AUSTIN
Just like a capitalist.

TERESA
It takes a professional.

*Walter counts out money to Alice, who
plays the banker.*

WALTER
That's why I got the wheelbarrow, so I can load my
dough into it.

ALICE
You gave me too much.

AUSTIN
Count your money, Walter. Alice, count his money
for him.

WALTER
This is too much like work for me. Why are we playing Monopoly?

ALICE
Austin, they don't want to play. It's after midnight.

AUSTIN
Sure they do.

ALICE
Let's just sit and talk.

TERESA
Walter, my dear, we are playing Monopoly because
you never leave a party when the other guests do.
You and Austin are dear old college roommates with
absolutely nothing to say to each other. And if Alice
and I were going to last into the wee hours we had
to resort to something.

WALTER
We used to talk in college. What did we talk about?

AUSTIN
If we were getting laid. And why I did and you
didn't. *(landing on a space)* No, I don't want that.

WALTER
Oh ho. We'd all be going out drinking, Austin sits
there, "You wanna come?" "No, Walter, I'm painting
the Mona Lisa," he says, no shit, "I think there's a
market for it." That was actually pretty funny, if
you stop to think. *(rolling)* Come on, doubles. I'm
gonna buy some houses.

> *He moves.*

Oh hell.

> *Pays a fine. Teresa pours wine from gallon
> jug. Alice declines. Others drink.*

No, sure, Austin's not all that interested in real estate investments, and I can't say I'm too curious
about the modern Pop Art. Or whatta they call it
now, Op Art? Slop Art? Flop Art?

TERESA
(landing) I'll buy it, I'll buy it.

AUSTIN
I gave you one of my paintings. Did you put it up?

WALTER
It's over the fridge. *(patting his belly)* Scares me
away.

TERESA
Alice, how you doing? Ok?

ALICE
I'm a housewife.

A hitch.

No, I'm sorry, what?—

TERESA
No, I know that. I mean, you don't have to be the
bank all the time. Take turns and you can play too.

ALICE
I like to do it. Keep it in little stacks.

AUSTIN
Alice has the right idea. Sit back and watch us
make asses of ourselves.

ALICE
I just prefer it.

AUSTIN
Like after college she gave up painting so I would be
the sole and only mediocre painter in the family.

Pause.

I don't think I meant that the way it sounded.
(drawing) Chance!

WALTER
No, seriously, you're doing ok, aren't you? Professor
of art?

AUSTIN
Assistant professor. Last semester I taught four
sections of Intro.

ALICE
(giggling) He almost got to the color green.

AUSTIN
That's her one joke. No, in the profession there is a
type known as the Flathead, who keeps coming up
for tenure and *(slapping the top of his head)* hitting
the ceiling.

WALTER
I'll set you up a franchise for basket-weaving.

TERESA
Walter!

AUSTIN
Thanks.

> *Walter laughs at his joke. They drink.*

WALTER
Why the hell are we playing Monopoly?

TERESA
I remember this marvelous game at a party once.
We were all drunk, and we made these totally outra-
geous deals: I'll give you this property in exchange
for rent control, or I'll perform an obscene act upon
you if you get me out of jail. It was ruthless.

WALTER
Aren't you gonna buy anything? What a loser.

AUSTIN
In time, Walter.

TERESA
Walter's buying everything on the board.

WALTER
Wait'll I start buying houses.

TERESA
(a quick hug) I always trust his business moves.

AUSTIN
What about . . . Strip Monopoly?

TERESA
Woo!

WALTER
No fair. Business majors never got to sit in class
naked like you artists did.

AUSTIN
We had to wear little baggies.

ALICE
Austin—

AUSTIN
Teresa, can you imagine Walter in a baggie?

WALTER
Never mind what she can imagine.

AUSTIN
Well you must have made *some* impression. How long you been together, six months? No impression?

ALICE
Austin, you're being crude.

AUSTIN
Teresa, in your job you meet all those stimulating authors? Why not give Walter the bum's rush?

TERESA
Writers! At least Walter takes a bath. Besides, we publish children's books.

AUSTIN
(moving) Monopoly is based on the Darwinian principle of the Survival of the Luckiest.

ALICE
You're on his property.

AUSTIN
He rolled! He didn't see me! I don't have to pay.

WALTER
(landing) Wait. I will buy it, I will.

TERESA
Yike! Park Place!

AUSTIN
Monopoly.

> *Walter clowns, cheering for himself, giggling maniacally, counting out money.*

TERESA
The handwriting's on the wall.

WALTER
Jesus, I don't have enough money. Wait. Yes I do. Ok. Here we go! Urban renewal!

> *He brandishes the deed.*

TERESA
Watch him grind us peasants into the dust.

WALTER
Look at that. I get a monopoly, and here I am without a pot to piss in.

> *He counts the few dollars he has left. Aus-*
> *tin draws a Chance card.*

AUSTIN
Each player pay me seventy-five dollars.

WALTER
Oh shit, I don't have it. Give me a refill. . .

> *Teresa pours. A new stage of intoxication:*
> *Walter surlier, Teresa sillier, Austin more*
> *focused, more impulsive, Alice more rigid.*

ALICE
You have to mortgage your property.

AUSTIN
The walking encyclopedia.

ALICE
I'm just saying—

AUSTIN
No I didn't mean to—

WALTER
Mortgage, hell. . .

AUSTIN
Wait a minute. Here's a deal. I've got the cash, I'll
go into partnership with you. You own the property,
I put up the cash to build, we split the rent and I am
immune from rent for the next five rounds. Was
that the sort of deal you were talking about, Teresa?

TERESA
That's it. Ouch.

WALTER
Ok. I'll crush her, then turn on you.

ALICE
You can't do that.

AUSTIN
The government can do anything.

ALICE
There isn't any government.

AUSTIN
Who's the government? The people. Who's the people? We're the people. So we vote on it.

ALICE
I think if we play we should follow the rules. Maybe
that's stupid.

AUSTIN
Yes, it is. I move that any rule can be suspended by
a majority vote.

WALTER
Second. All in favor? *(with Austin)* Aye!

They look at Teresa.

TERESA
Ok, I'll be a sport. Aye.

AUSTIN
All opposed?

ALICE
Never mind.

AUSTIN
Ok. Now we're going to put three houses on Boardwalk and three on Park Place. And we're going to
watch Teresa land there on her next move. One two
three: roll'em!

She rolls. Squeals:

TERESA
Oh no! I did!

WALTER
Pay up.

TERESA
I thought we were friends.

WALTER
Oh we are. But business is business.

> *He pounds table, clowning. She starts to
> count out bills in two stacks.*

AUSTIN
Ok. Wait. Here. You pay him half. Right. Good.
Now I'll propose a deal. You can keep what you owe
me. On one condition.

TERESA
I'll take it, I'll take it!

AUSTIN
That I must approve any and all deals whatever
that you'd make with Walter. No ganging up on me.

WALTER
Don't be dumb. That's the only protection you got.

TERESA
It's a deal.

AUSTIN
Now I'll propose another deal—

ALICE
Austin—

AUSTIN
I've found my true calling. Now, Walter, I will give
you my interest in the high-rent district, including
the houses, in return for your deed to Kentucky Avenue, provided I keep my immunity.

WALTER
Throw in the cash for hotels and it's a deal.

AUSTIN
Oh, you're draining me. You're such a tiger. Ok.

ALICE
(counting them out) Hotels.

AUSTIN
Now, Teresa, I propose another deal—

WALTER
Hey, shut up and play.

AUSTIN
Walter, I'm playing. I'm sitting here with my feet
on the desk, and I'm making phone calls, and I'm
making it all happen, and I'm rewarded by getting
rich. Isn't that how it's done? Isn't that the dream?

TERESA
Yes, Austin?

AUSTIN
I will now combine Kentucky Avenue with your two red properties to form a monopoly—

WALTER
Hey!

AUSTIN
Under the same terms I had with Walter. Split the loot.

WALTER
See, he's just playing us off against one another!

TERESA
(to Walter) Can you make me a better deal?

AUSTIN
Ah hah! I cannot *consent* to any better deal.

TERESA
It's a deal.

AUSTIN
(to Alice, flamboyantly) See? Little did you guess. Disguised as a mild-mannered assistant professor of art, I fight the never-ending battle for monopoly, moolah, and the American Way!

ALICE
Do tell.

> *He freezes, stung by the perceived sarcasm. Walter shuffles through his deeds.*

TERESA
Hey listen, troops, I think we're all getting a little tired of this. So either we need to get a whole lot drunker or let's do something else.

AUSTIN
Stop me before I kill again.

WALTER
Never let it be said that some half-baked little art-fart out-wolfed the Wolf of Wall Street. Let the game go on.

TERESA
Here goes the bloodbath.

ALICE
Just play it for fun. I mean, can't you just play it for
fun?

WALTER
(rolling dice) Shit!

> *The game and the drinking continue, as*
> *Austin and Alice alternately speak front,*
> *telling us the story, turning back to the*
> *game as the other continues.*

AUSTIN
(front) I had the time of my life. All the time hearing how much money he's making, and he's in the
real world and I'm in the ivory tower, and here he is
like a big turd in the frying pan—

ALICE
(front) It was really cruel. I can't stand it when he
drinks. Like he thinks he's so clever. There's people in the department that won't speak to us because of something he said at parties, like he was
biting back—

AUSTIN
(front) It was absolutely wild. I got a magic marker
and drew a tollway past Jail: pay or take a chance.
I subdivided property, got zoning variances to build
casinos. I even drew properties on the inside of the
board, called it landfill—

ALICE
(front) The rest were as bad as he was, like it was
real—

AUSTIN
(front) We converted the Go square to a public au-
thority, so when somebody passed Go the money
went into a fund, which I controlled, for the purpose
of public improvements . . . on my properties.

ALICE
(front) If I'd been playing he would have turned on
me, try to say things that hurt. In a very clever
way.

AUSTIN
(front) They kept going backrupt, but my finance company just floated loans, so they couldn't die, they just kept hanging there on the spikes.

ALICE
(front) I still think he loves me, but he doesn't have much talent for it.

AUSTIN
(front) Don't ask me why they didn't just up and quit. Things take their own rhythm. It was all quite real.

> *Time has passed. All are very drunk, caught in the game. Alice brings another jug of wine to the table. Teresa opens it and pours. Walter rolls dice, moves, lands.*

WALTER
You bastard.

AUSTIN
Sticks and stones will break my bones but names will cost you money. Can't pay? How about a deal?

TERESA
Don't make him deals, Walter, let's you and I make the deals, and— I have not been this drunk for a very . . . quite of a while . . . Woo!

AUSTIN
Walter, isn't it a shame that you need money, and sweet Teresa with the tits needs money, and there's all that pile of hot money over there by ambivalent Alice not doing an old thing.

WALTER
Son of a bitch. . .

AUSTIN
Let's work it this way. Samuel Johnson, an old English phony, said one day, just off the top of his head, "There is an appeal from art to reality." So this is reality. We take over the bank. Ok, Alice? We create a holding company to hold us the bank.

ALICE
Don't be silly.

AUSTIN
All right, we won't be silly. All in favor.

OTHERS
Aye.

TERESA
Alice, it's just a game. . .

ALICE
I'm the bank!

AUSTIN
Locked up tight.

ALICE
Ok, deal me out.

AUSTIN
Ok, deal her out. Here's your severance pay. We'll give you a gold watch. Ok, here's five hundred for you, five hundred for me, five hundred for you—

ALICE
You and your goddamn game!

> *She knocks her wine over on the table: a
> strangled, spasmodic attempt to attack.*

WALTER
It's all over the money. . .

AUSTIN
Hurricane Alice has struck the coast.

TERESA
The mad bomber!

AUSTIN
Five hundred for you, five hundred for you—

ALICE
Austin, stop it!

AUSTIN
It's ok, Alice, I have no pride, I married you. That's not a personal insult, that's just something I thought of saying. Let's vote Alice into jail.

WALTER
I can't find my hotel—

AUSTIN
The first orange taffeta militant.

TERESA
Alice, it's ok, it's a game—

AUSTIN
Into the slammer.

THREE
Aye.

AUSTIN
You're the flatiron. You're in jail.

ALICE
I'm not the flatiron! I'm here!

AUSTIN
She's not ready for parole. Negative attitude.

TERESA
It's just a game, Alice, we're the same people—

AUSTIN
She's kidding. She does this. Your turn, Walter.

WALTER
Whatever I do, I'm screwed.

AUSTIN
Hey Walter, I don't want that. You don't have to be
screwed. How bout if it's Teresa. I mean, we're old
buddies, Walter. You be district vice president of
the Baltic Avenue division, vice president in charge
of the vices of the president! You keep your marker
right there, you don't even move, and hey Walter,
you'll work up, right up the board, right up to
Boardwalk! Boardwalk! Hey, and we'll take care of
that little lady, Walter, all the best hotels. Cause I
see this great system . . . and everybody knows their
place . . . everybody's worth so much. . . and they
know their place . . . and this whole . . . godawful
game can . . . STOP! Oh Jesus Christ. . .

TERESA
Walter, let's go—

> *Confused, he shoves her away. Austin
> starts to embrace her, barely able to stand.*

Walter sees him, starts pounding on him
luggishly, in an absurdly incompetent
attempt to fight.

WALTER
Bastard. . . Son of a bitch. . . You bastard. . .

ALICE
(screaming) It's all done!

She sweeps the board off the table. Walter
releases Austin, leans heavily on a chair.
Teresa cries out. Tumult dies. Teresa sobs,
trying to control herself. Alice stands rigid.
Austin fumbles to adjust his glasses.

AUSTIN
I'm not like that. . . It was just what we start into
doing. . . It's just a game. . . It isn't real. . . We're
still the same people we were. . . All the deals. . . I
deeply believe in non-violence, and we might have
disagreements but. . . Children's books, and serious
artworks, and sure, even real estate, there's a human factor, I think. . . Oh Jesus Christ. . .

He stumbles among them, touches them as
if to repair the damage. Holds Alice in a
sluggish embrace.

ALICE
I'll make the coffee.

Fade.

Part Four
CLOSE-OUT SALES

The very idea of theatre, like love-making, carries a terror with it: the terror of presence, of being alive enough to risk high stakes. While the Lottery allows colossal gain with minimal investment — against truly farcical odds — neither Real Life nor Theatre works that way. Which perhaps explains why neither calling is now as popular as the Lottery.

One Sunday in November '82, we sat around a littered table in a back room at the Baltimore Theatre Project (amid renovations that, after years of struggle, marked its elevation from shoestring to high-button shoes) — with a half dozen friends. We were frayed old colleagues, the debris of each other's past, actors, playwrights, all full of love for one another and anxiety about the future of serious theatre in America. Is it doomed? What does it signify that there's much more serious criticism written on popular movies and rock than on drama? That nobody rushes out to buy a copy of this year's Pulitzer Prize play, and few remember its name? What's the place of art in a world of pesticides that don't faze the pests? Of course, when we said *theatre*, we meant *us*.

But the fact is, despite our justifiable paranoia, that living theatre still exists, having survived plague, moralists and movies. It may even survive gentility. Theatre exists to bring us into *intense presence*. To sit with the assembled members of the tribe — in body paint, feathers, togas, doublets, blue jeans or business garb — and celebrate the grief and silliness, pain and promise, surprise and sunlight of being human. Most of us settle into premature senility about the age of five, and while this is undeniably cost-effective, it's really a damned shame.

About the time of this stern conclusion, the clock hands drooped and the wine jug gurgled its death gulp. Our young son, who had been scribbling out slips of paper in the bare corner, circulated among us and handed them out, one to each of his assembled but disintegrating elders. *"This is a ticket to Here, Right Now."* And it was.

All the following acts are about Death and our elaborate strategies to avoid answering the door. Even the jack-hammer litany of **Questions** reserves that malignant pause at the squat of the question mark when no reply is forthcoming. Some apology is usually expected when writing about morbidity. Maybe the old saw serves best: unless we breathe the gamy stink of Death, we can't begin to lick Life's juicy face. Nearly everyone dies, even serial killers and critics, and we might define a Comedy as any play where we forget to come back for the final act. So we don't feel we're obliged to apologize for Death: we write about it, but it wasn't our idea.

In fact, we would suggest that these acts, for live performance, are best approached in the spirit of *commedia*, the popular comedy that had fullest flower in 17th Century Italy and one of its countless reincarnations in Chaplin: funny yet moving, artificial yet real, loveable yet mean, hungry in gut yet overwhelmingly bountiful in comic spirit.

Why *commedia* as a model for staging morbid nightmare? Arlecchino tries to consume his own hand because he's *genuinely* starving, yet despite hideous pain he eats it as delicately as his hunger allows, since he's also a gourmet. Pantalone, distraught, tries to lie down and die in peace, but he keeps farting — a terribly distracting accompaniment to suicide. Life's most pressing emergencies are crystallized in incongruity; life *is* incongruity.

So we never hold a single mood for long: we jiggle our brimming jigger of hemlock, and it stains our best new sweater. In **Condemned**, Camilla's wrenching vision of a paved-over wasteland is interrupted by a phone call. In **Doom**, the vaudeville team runs rampant, yet the terror they broadcast is what made the Lottery line in downtown Gettysburg, during our most recent visit there, nearly two blocks long — testing whether that nation, or any nation so conceived and so dedicated, can long endure. The terrified duo of **The Shadow** will most likely outlast any real medical emergency, even the hackneyed campfire skit they dream, to face — as we did — the mundane nightmare of paying hospital bills. It's the stuff of pure comedy.

How incongruous, how exasperatingly inelegant, in plays about Death, to *survive*.

CONDEMNED

In the field of a nightmare. Ticking. Distant hospital sounds. Footsteps in echoing hallway. Low, anxious chattering, whispering, laughter. A woman walks down into sharp light. Stands, waiting for us to notice her. Clears her throat.

CAMILLA

Excuse me. My name is Camilla Leonard, and I've been condemned.

Gasp. Slowly, light up on a distant figure at a microphone: the M.C. Or there are many M.C.'s at mikes, speaking in unison.

They told me to see the Board. Are you the Board?

Mumble.

Because they said if I expected to get anything out of you I must be dreaming. So I . . . must be dreaming. Are you the Board?

Mumble.

Because I got this notice, and they're going to tear me down. I don't know, they found some bleeding, or something in the connections, maybe the plumbing, or maybe I'm just past forty. So I want to apply for, what do you call it, a variance, where you give me some time to bring myself up to the building code. Because there are hazards, I know that. I have these depressions, but nothing serious. My family's not worried. I'm just sailing along.

Mumble.

But I do want to correct whatever violations there are, because I'm still structurally sound, and they say the older models are really in the prime of life, if you have enough heat. . .

She tries to laugh, sobs. Controls herself.

So I wrote out this formal request. Should I read it out? Are you the Board?

*She reaches into her shopping bag, pulls
out sheets from a roll of paper towels, continuing to unroll it, attempting to read
what's not written on it.*

It goes, "Whereas I am a citizen with rights apper-
taining thereto—" It's hard to see it—

M.C.
Sorry.

CAMILLA
And "lived numerous years without discredit—"
Could I sit down?

M.C.
No chair.

CAMILLA
A stool. Could I have a stool? How about the floor?

M.C.
Not in the cards.

CAMILLA
"And whereas—" Maybe a job.

M.C.
Very risky.

CAMILLA
I had one, but it doesn't fit the way it used to.

M.C.
No can do.

CAMILLA
"And whereas—" Can I visit my mother?

M.C.
No mother.

CAMILLA
Could I have a mother?

M.C.
Not just now.

CAMILLA
"And whereas—" See, it just feels like a kind of
lump, and everyone's been very understanding, I
think it's just me— Please look at me.

M.C.
Nope. No way. Nohow. No can do. Nosireebob.

CAMILLA
"Be it therefore resolved that I WANT A BETTER
DEAL!"

Pause.

Please?

M.C.
Say please.

CAMILLA
I said please.

M.C.
"Please."

CAMILLA
Please!

M.C.
Come to Santa.

> *Recorded ho-ho's. Woman moves to new*
> *area, tries to sit in a nonexistent lap.*

What do you want for Christmas, little girl?

CAMILLA
What can I have?

M.C.
How about a nosebleed?

CAMILLA
You're not the Board. You're here for the demolition.

> *Phone rings.*

I'll get it.

M.C.
Camilla. . .

> *She reaches for a phone, far distant. It con-*
> *tinues to ring as she reaches, calls to it.*

CAMILLA
Hi, Sue? Yeh, I just have to talk. I know you're tied
up, but— Jennifer, turn down the TV— Well, I had

the tests, but they won't say. It just feels like a
lump. You know when you don't get invited, there's
kind of a lump?

    M.C.
Camilla. . .

    CAMILLA
I don't even smoke. What does it mean, a spot on
the lung? It might just be tension. Tense lungs.
Oh, the doctor? I told him, "I will pray to the Holy
Virgin that you be maimed for life in a three-car
crash." No, that's terrible, I don't mean that. I'm
signalling. Nobody sees me signalling. I don't want
this exit ramp.

    M.C.
Camilla. . .

    CAMILLA
What if they fire me? It's not fair. A doctor can't
fire a patient. He can put them on hold, but he can't
disconnect.

    M.C.
Camilla. . .

    CAMILLA
They're all alive, and they're listening to music,
they've all got candy, they melt in your mouth, and
they're going to parties, they passed all their tests,
Chris, Jennifer, Trina, Mark. And *I'm* the one. I'm
the one with the lump!

    M.C.
Camilla. . .

    CAMILLA
I've never felt so much like . . . grabbing myself by
the throat. . . YOU TELL'EM OUT THERE. I'VE GOT
A HOSTAGE. I'VE GOT HER BY THE THROAT AND
THESE ARE MY DEMANDS. ONE, I WANT A BETTER
DEAL. TWO, I WANT SAFE PASSAGE. A BOEING
SEVEN FORTY-SEVEN TO . . . someplace safe. . .

    Silence. She stops reaching, looks at us.

Excuse me. My name is Camilla. And I'm lost. And
I want to go home.

She walks into a new area, as if through fog. Looks about in wonder.

I'm home. Hey. I'm home. It's been years. Oh, Mama told me, you go out there, they slam the door. Solitary confinement. Death row on a thirty-year mortgage. Oh, it's so nice to. . . Mama? Dad? I'm gonna curl up over by the fireplace. There's the fireplace, right next to the parking garage.

Startled pause.

I don't remember a parking garage in the living room. They changed things around. Maybe she's in the kitchen. She used to say, "This is like a freeway through here." Now there's a freeway . . . through the kitchen?

Looks about, panicked.

Hey, who messed up the place? Dad? Oh, there was a neat place you could hide, behind the sofa. It's still there! *(reading sign)* "Adult Books and Novelty Items. . ." No, the big chair, the arms were all worn off, I'll get up in it and snuggle in. . . Where's the chair? Where's the— Urban renewal. Franchises. Freeways. Demolition. No, this is wrong! Daddy! Mama! I want an exit ramp! I am gonna scream. I'm really gonna scream. I am now gonna scream.

Screams, but manages only a very, very tiny, constricted squeak.

I can't hear. There must be a power failure.

Phone rings. She is confused, looks about, as if waking. Sees the phone on a table at a distance. Walks over, answers it: reality.

Oh hi. Fine. No, I've got something I can heat up. What time will you be? Love you too. Oh, the doctor called, and then I dozed off. Well, they want to do some more tests. Two weeks. But I don't think it's anything, I haven't really felt much. Kind of a lump. Ok. Love you too. Bye.

Hangs up.

Love you.

Fade.

The earliest version of **Questions** was written in 1975, when we needed a second revue in our touring repertory and did our best to follow the formula of the first. We'd found that **Dreamers** — the litany of "I want's" — was an excellent opener, and since we were expending great creativity in van maintenance, diaper-changing, tour booking and general survival, we cut a few corners when it came to pioneering new conceptual modalities.

But we found that we were lousy self-plagiarizers. Some good sketches came out of the show, **SUNSHINE BLUES** (which seems to have contributed its name, belatedly, to a Philadelphia fashion boutique), but the show itself had a limp spine. It takes real skill to follow formulae, to tread over well-trodden ground looking for stray bucks; that's the essence of commercial work, and we respect it when it's not utterly sleazy. But we discovered we had little skill in doing that: we were saved from mediocrity by a lack of talent.

Questions soon died a death-by-file-folder. It was rewritten entirely for **HEART'S DESIRE** in 1988 and performed with four actors. With reassignment of some lines, it can be played by casts ranging from two to a dozen, but it demands, above all, actors who can play rapid tempo while striking each key with direct, sweaty reality. Movements and regroupings are useful to the extent that they clarify the structure, but the piece tends to stimulate extravagantly creative stage-craft that then requires a lot of work to simplify back to skin and bones.

Like **Dreamers**, the sketch is a collage of theme-and-variations. Its simple premise — asking questions without getting answers — makes no profound statement. Whatever we get from it, we get in fragments. Its unity comes solely from the characters' need for real answers. For the actor, it presents the very difficult task of asking silly questions without telegraphing to the audience that they're silly. It may be useful for each performer to write out, privately, a list of the questions for which, at one time or another, answers were most urgently desired. In what tone of voice, with what degree of assertiveness or hesitancy, would *these* be asked? Without that personal connection, the litany will become coy or cloying. The proper tone of absurdity can breed, generate and mature only in a tepid sea of dead seriousness.

QUESTIONS

*A quartet of actors in a maze of chairs.
They speak singly and together — to
themselves, to each other, or to us — transforming from character to character.*

Who.
What.
Where.
When.
How.
Which.
Why.

WHY?

Why does it snow?
Why Evelyn why?
Why didn't you call?
Why do I snore?

WHERE?

Where's the men's room?
Where does God sleep?
Where's my mommy?

WHO?

Who didn't flush?
Who killed Kennedy?
Who is The Real Me?
Who cares?

WHAT?

What are the chief exports of Uruguay?
What is the proper end of man?
What hath God wrought?
What do you do for gas?

HOW?

How's it going?

How am I gonna cope?

How do you commit adultery?

Good question.

Well it's hard to explain.

I'm glad you asked.

> *Silence. Then they shift abruptly, as in*
> *Musical Chairs. Each sits alone, brooding.*

What if I work real hard and do all my homework
and learn the stuff so I get good grades and know all
kinds of stuff, then can I forget it?

What if I grow up and I get married and we buy a
house and have to pay the bank a lot of money so I
go to work every day and the furnace breaks down
and I don't know how to fix it because they never
tell you that, and everybody says "You're the daddy,
what are you going to do?" — What about that?

Why can't you just go up to a person and ask whatever you want to ask and it's a law they have to tell
you the answer and it's the right answer and they
won't make fun of you for asking and they won't tell
your mom that you asked and the answer isn't
something you really don't want to hear?

> *All shift. A young couple, holding hands,*
> *try to find words. Young man blurts out:*

Have you ever said "I love you"?

Who would I say it to?

Well, who's your favorite movie star?

Who's yours?

What's on your mind?

What time is it getting to be?

(aside) How do you seduce somebody? Does she
want me to come on strong? Has she ever done it
before? What do you do afterward? What if I'm not
endowed enough?

(aside) How do you seduce somebody? Should I smile more? Why not tonight? Why do I have to go to the bathroom *now*? What if I really got pregnant? Why can't I say what's on my mind?

Silence. He speaks:

Need to get home early?

Do you mind?

Shift. Kid stands in the center. Others sit in thoughtful postures.

No, wait, I really want some answers. I want to get to the bottom of this. I really want to know.

I'm sure we all do.

I mean, give me the real lowdown.

Story behind the headlines.

Well, it's a beautiful answer. See, when two people love each other very much, and they get married and promise to be true, then they become a mommy and daddy, and they sleep in the same bed, and there's just so much love that it makes a little baby, and they name him Kenneth, and that's how it is.

I already heard that one.

All right. It's because Daddy has to work very hard all day, and money isn't just something you buy candy with, it's something that buys food to make us grow up big and strong so we can get a good job and make money so we can grow up big and strong and that's all you need to know.

No it's not. It hurts. The question mark has a hook, so it sticks and you can't get it loose. I gotta know. Exactly how much is the cost of living? Is there a Santa Claus? What happens after you die? What happens before you die? Why can't we have lots of big orgies? Who was that masked man anyhow? Where's the valley of death? Do miracles happen? What is truth?

Shift. All focus on a statuesque figure.

Breathes there a man with soul so dead
Who never to himself hath said—
What does she look like naked?

> *Shift. A couple, the woman pregnant. She*
> *speaks, half to herself.*

Boy or a girl, you think?

One or the other.

What if there's something the matter?

Know where I put my coffee cup?

What if he's three years old and he runs out into the
street and I don't see it in time and there's a bus
and he's screaming but at least he's alive—

Dja hear me?

And we get in the car and we think he's ok but on
the way to the hospital I look in his eyes and he isn't
there any more—

Wasn't it there?

Or what if there's one baby after another and they
all grow up healthy, they all have babies, we celebrate Thanksgiving but there's a little some kind of
chemical in the turkey—

You think it tastes funny?

Or little metallic slivers in the air, maybe something
we gave them years ago for the chicken pox and it
starts to work and it grows and it works and we
open the Christmas presents and find—

Something wrong?

How can you ask me that?

What else can I say?

Why do you turn everything into a question?

How does that make you feel?

> *Shift. All desperate to find the answer*
> *somewhere:*

No, I want a straight answer. Plain English. Cards
on the table.

Verbatim et literatim.

Great ocean of truth.

Ask and ye shall be given.

Tell me.

Tell me straight out.

The straight scoop.

The naked truth.

Just the facts.

Cut the doubletalk.

Please?

Pretty please?

Why? Why do I have to study?

Why do I have to say please?

Why do I have to change my clothes?

Why do I have to mow the grass?

Why do I have to be nice?

Why do I have to kiss ass?

Why do I have to grin and bear it?

Why do I have to use Desenex daily?

Why do I have to see it all disappear?

Why do I have to ask why?

Why do I have to live so long? Why do I have to be alone? Why do I have to see it all disappear?

Why do I have to. . . Why *do* I have to?

Why? Why do I *have* to?

Why?

Why?

There are no easy answers.

> *Long pause. All speak in unison, very quietly, with great trepidation:*

Why?

> *Fade, with no answer forthcoming.*

Doom was written for **THE MONEY SHOW**, a Chicago debacle in 1975, and revised for **THE WANT ADS**, a Lancaster reject in 1984. It's about that rush of adrenalin that comes every time the phone rings when it shouldn't. And it's about the odd shame and humiliation that accompany the experience of being a loser — paradoxically greater if it's not your own fault. It may be helpful to think of it less as a revue sketch and more as a three-voice poem for the stage: all three creatures are aspects of a single shaky dreamer.

The Shadow emerged after the experience of a long hospitalization — a waking nightmare that mixed rage at the medical profession with a reluctant understanding that these people, whatever their flaws, were saving one's life. Bits of it are based on work as a bookkeeper in 1966 for a California internist who was also a sensitive, caring, driven *mensch*. So although it contains moments of vengeance, it's not intended as a satire on doctors. It's more an unsettled meditation on the amazing penchant of human beings to embrace Life, an invariably fatal disease.

Stuff We're Saving Up was written for **BLACK DOG** in 1978, based on improvisations by Camilla Schade and Joe Uher, but its seed was a Theatre X skit — left half-baked — about a group at a bus-stop, each proudly carrying a large cardboard box having no function other than its status as *possession*. It drew also on an indelible undergraduate memory of Chicago mime Bud Beyer in a "walking through life" sketch. Performers would do well to spend one rehearsal using cans full of ripe garbage. They're not carrying a poetic conceit; they're toting pure rot.

While these acts demand close interplay, there is again a sense of animals trapped in headlights, unable to dodge, unable to look away. The vague, amorphous yet overwhelming Presence is out front, drawing the actors into "presentation" no matter how much they would prefer to create their own insulated stage world. Behind the adult's goggle eyes is the child-self stark naked in the chill examining room: "I'm here. It's happening. There's no way out."

Still, these people are quite courageous. They play out their scenes, knowing we're watching, knowing we won't give them a damn bit of help, and that when it's time to write their obituary, they'll probably be panned by the drama critic. They don't complain.

DOOM

*Fragments of a working-class living room.
Nelly vacuums the carpet. Sharp door
buzzer. She turns off the vacuum, hurries
to answer the door. Opening it, she finds
herself face-to-face with two heavy men
wearing identical trench coats and derbies.
They raise their hands in unison, waving to
her, then tipping their hats. Machine-gun
rhythm:*

JONES

Mrs. Bird? We're the Messengers of Doom.

NELLY

I don't understand.

SMITH

Course not. That's why Mr. Jones asked me to
join him. Cause we want to do our best to answer
whatever questions you may have.

JONES

Sure to be some.

SMITH

No question.

NELLY

Are you selling something?

JONES

Mr. Smith means that we're the Messengers of
Doom.

SMITH

Could we step in?

JONES

Ample identification.

SMITH

More than enough.

JONES

Clear as day.

SMITH
Testimonials.

JONES
Revelations and prophecies.

SMITH
Step right in.

JONES
Why thanks.

SMITH
You're welcome.

> *One honks a horn. They sweep past her to*
> *the center of the room, stop, tip hats.*

Mrs. Bird, I'd like to ask you a personal question.
You have, I suppose, heard of a Mr. Richard Bird?

NELLY
That's my husband.

JONES
Congratulations. I hadn't heard. Are you happy?

SMITH
Shut up. Mrs. Bird, I'm afraid in that case we have
some bad news. Are you ready?

JONES
We're the Messengers of Doom.

SMITH
Shut up. Would you like to sit down?

NELLY
What's the matter?

SMITH
What's the matter! You're standing up! Would you
like to sit down!

JONES
(sitting) Don't mind if I do!

SMITH
(to Jones) Stand up!

JONES
(rising, to Nelly) Siddown!

BOTH
(forcing her down in the chair) SIDDOWN!

    Silence.

SMITH
Ok. Mrs. Bird, I don't know how to tell you this, but
without beating around the bush, without shilly-
shallying, without hemming and hawing, without
giving you some kinda song and dance, without a
moment's hesitation, while you were just sitting
there without a care in the world, Mr. Bird has
snapped.

NELLY
What?

JONES
Snapped.

SMITH
Like a snapper.

JONES
Snap.

SMITH
Mr. Bird has snapped.

JONES
Doom.

    She starts to rise. They push her down.

BOTH
SIDDOWN!

SMITH
Mrs. Bird, let me fill you in. Your husband has been
under strain. A lot of it's money. You buy things.
Say instead of being the Messengers of Doom, we
were selling magazines, I'd look at you and I'd say,
"That's an easy mark." Now he's been working aw-
fully hard, I mean that his company has had to lay a
lot of people off to make ends meet, and he's had to
work overtime, which he's done, God bless him, say
seventeen or eighteen hours a day, cause those ends
have got to meet. And the money crunch has been
hard on you too, where you haven't always been in
the mood to fulfill your marital duty, as they say.

And he's upset, he's under strain and he's tried to
get a little tail around the office but no luck because
most of the tail has been laid off. So he snapped.

JONES

We come to tell you.

NELLY

I don't understand, he had a nervous breakdown or
what? Where is he? In the hospital or—

SMITH

Mrs. Bird, don't be so concerned, cause that ain't the
worst. Would you sign this paper, please?

NELLY

What is it?

SMITH

Sign it! What does it look like? It's a paper!

BOTH

SIDDOWN!

> *They shove her down. Dead silence.*

NELLY

Could you. . . If you could just tell me. . .

JONES

(stage whisper) That ain't all. It Ain't All!

SMITH

Cause have we got news for you!

JONES

Doom.

SMITH

Mrs. Bird, you have a father, right? Your father's
retired. He's vulnerable. He's living on Social Security, right? Fixed income, vulnerable to inflation
and emphysema. Mrs. Bird, you put him in a nursing home. I know, you thought that was the best
thing, cause maybe you'd have to go out working
and you couldn't stay home and change his diapers,
I know. But you must have heard.

JONES

Hark.

SMITH

You've heard of nursing homes that starve the old gentlemen. You've seen it on TV. They drug the old ladies, they don't let'em have babies, they take away their Wheaties and they let'em shrivel up. You've read all about it.

NELLY

No.

SMITH

Well, your dad got in with a bad lot. Have a cigar.

JONES

Thanks.

SMITH

Shut up. They sat down to supper. Seven hungry codgers and three ravenous crones. Your father was hard of hearing, and when they told him what they were going to do, he said, "Carry on!"

JONES

Gave his consent.

SMITH

In writing.

JONES

Unconditional.

SMITH

They boiled him.

JONES

Boiled your dad.

SMITH

Served him up.

JONES

Worcestershire Sauce.

SMITH

Lasted three weeks.

JONES

Doom doom doom.

SMITH

Course we heard.

JONES
Sympathized.

SMITH
No hard feelings.

JONES
In memoriam.

SMITH
Gave his all.

JONES
Paid the price.

SMITH
Roll on thou deep and dark blue ocean roll.

JONES
Missing in action.

SMITH
Absent with leave.

NELLY
Stop it! Are you crazy? I don't understand what you're saying. I don't understand—

SMITH
Course you don't. And there's reasons for that.

JONES
Maybe you're dumb.

SMITH
So we're here to tell you so then you'll know what you don't understand.

JONES
Gimme a dollar.

NELLY
No!

JONES
You don't understand.

SMITH
You certainly don't understand.

NELLY
I'm going to scream.

JONES
Gimme a dollar.

SMITH
Dollar a scream.

JONES
Quarter a squeal.

SMITH
Wait! Don't scream! That ain't the worst! Don't
you want to hear the worst? How am I gonna tell
you the worst if you're screaming while I tell you?

JONES
Doom.

> *Silence. She sits slowly, frozen. They try
> various grave theatrical stances, prolong-
> ing the delay. Then they speak.*

SMITH
Mrs. Bird, you have a little boy. You love your little
boy. You ain't got a barrel of money, but love makes
up for a lot. Well I'll tell you—

JONES
Or I'll tell her—

SMITH
I'll tell her!

JONES
Doom.

SMITH
Your little boy got an ow-ey. Got an ow-ey in his
tummy. They had to take him to fix his tummy, but
then they couldn't. Why? He hadn't established a
credit rating. Course not, he's only five years old.
He can't buy a car, he can't take out a loan, he has
absolutely no way to demonstrate that the hospital
could expect any compensation for removal of the
ow-ey other than the profound and heartfelt glow of
Christian charity, which just won't hack it. So your
little boy, Mrs. Bird, has reached a dead end.

JONES
Ground Zero.

SMITH
Lost Horizons.

JONES
Call of the Wild.

NELLY
Stop it! Tell me!

JONES
Gimme a dollar.

SMITH
Where is it?

JONES
Up your garter?

SMITH
Down your bazoom?

JONES
Dollar dollar dollar.

BOTH
Doom!

NELLY
What's happened to my son!

SMITH
Pardon the question, but are you incorporated? If
you are, you can include an indemnification clause
which would cover whatever your board decided was
proper, assuming he was engaged in the business of
the corporation, which you define in your articles.
I'd recommend it.

JONES
No, Sid. Then it's subject to windfall. You can't
beat windfall.

*From somewhere, sentimental music as
Smith becomes philosophical.*

SMITH
But whatta you do if you've tried it all?
You read all the bestsellers: Melt Away Inches
    While You Sleep. One Hundred Proven Ways to
    Make a Million. Fifty Cents a Day Buys Life
    After Death.

You sent for those Tips on Kitchen Magic. You sent
for Slim Whitman's Greatest Hits, but he didn't
tell you a thing.

You tried to find the answers, you bought a Home
Family Encyclopedia, only fifteen dollars per
week, the answers to everything except where
you get the fifteen dollars a week.

You tried to open the free sample, but you couldn't
get through the plastic: you tore at it, ripped it,
bit it, hammered it, finally threw it out, and
then you got the bill.

You thought, "What if I change my name?" You
thought, "What if I rapidly die?" You thought,
"What if I build a more powerful vocabulary and
identify the erogenous zones and diversify my
holdings of stocks and bonds and find exciting
new uses for home computers and become truly
liberated and discover the power of prayer and
look out for Number One?"

But whatta you do?

Whatta you do if you stare at the wall?

Whatta you do if you can't find the switch?

Whatta you do if some clowns show up at the door?

Whatta you do?

JONES
You're screwed.

SMITH
See, Mrs. Bird, we just want to let you know how
the system works.

JONES
Not very damn well.

SMITH
Cause you don't know how the system works.

JONES
You're at the mercy.

SMITH
Raw meat.

JONES
Sitting duck.

SMITH
Hoodwinked and bamboozled.

JONES
Stunned and befuddled.

SMITH
Duped and abused.

She cries out, collapses. Long pause.

In point of fact, there is some hope.

NELLY
I don't understand.

SMITH
Course not. I wouldn't expect you to. And it's not
very interesting anyway, all full of technical jargon,
graphs and charts and decimal points.

JONES
It's your choice.

SMITH
It's your choice. You can take time to scour through
a library of books and try to understand what's baf-
fled the best minds of our time, it's your choice.

JONES
Or—

SMITH
Or you can make a better choice. Here it is.

JONES
Gimme a dollar.

SMITH
Sunny side of the street.

JONES
Happy ending.

SMITH
Life is a cabaret old chum.

BOTH
The Lottery!

SMITH
Your chance of a lifetime.

JONES
Your place in the sun.

SMITH
Your last best hope. Think of it. One buck, and you
could be sitting pretty. Unsnap your hubby, sew up
your little boy, and set up a polished memorial tab-
let to your daddy who has met a fate approximately
equivalent to death.

JONES
See, we don't want to be the Messengers of Doom.

SMITH
No way.

JONES
We'd rather be the Harbingers of Hope.

BOTH
(carried away) Hope! Hope! Hope! Hope hop heep
hipe! Hope! Hope!

NELLY
Stop!

They freeze mid-frolic, regain dignity.

SMITH
All right, Mrs. Bird. O-kaaaay. . . You think you'll
wake up. It's all a dream, right? Just one of those
crazy dreams? Sure it is. Sure you will. You'll
wake up. And then you'll be awake. And then it
won't be a dream. And you still won't understand.

JONES
And that's a fact.

SMITH
That's the long and the short.

JONES
That's all she wrote.

SMITH
Until we shall meet.

JONES
Again.

*They have retreated to the door with ges-
tures of leave-taking. At the last word, they
slam it shut. Nelly is frozen.*

NELLY
I'll turn on the—

> *She makes a vague gesture toward the TV
> but can't move. Silence.*

Wait. Is that what you're selling? Lottery tickets?
Sure, I'll buy one, if it's only a dollar, you never
know.   Some guy in Allentown, he'd been out of
work three months, he'll never have to worry. They
say there's always hope. Is there some kind of special deal? I don't understand.

> *At one side, the vacuum cleaner starts in
> full whine. She looks at it. Lights fade.*

THE SHADOW

Mort and Mara in nightclothes, getting into bed, adjusting pillows, bantering but very edgy.

MORT
Beddy-bye.

MARA
When do we have to get up?

MORT
When's your appointment?

MARA
Nine. Then I'll bring the car back and you go for yours.

MORT
Why'd you make our checkups on the same day?

MARA
That way everything's done.

MORT
Suppose we're both sick?

MARA
If you're sick you're sick.

MORT
If I know it I'm sicker.

MARA
You had too much to drink.

MORT
Alcohol sterilizes. My germs are clean.

MARA
They'll look inside you and find pickled gut.

MORT
Put your sick mind to sleep.

MARA
I feel strange.

MORT
(settling in) Get some sleep, honey.

MARA
(settling in) Don't act like my doctor.

> *Pause. Instant shift of worlds: He stands upright, looming over her. She sits, rigid.*

MORT
Hello, I'm your doctor. How do you feel?

MARA
All right.

MORT
Headaches? Hallucinations?

MARA
No.

MORT
Pain? Constipation?

MARA
No.

MORT
How old are your parents? Epilepsy? Seizures?
Searches? When did you have a bath?

MARA
Never.

MORT
What did they tell you in school? Do you like the
feel of cotton sheets? Can you take criticism? Dizzy
spells? Ringworm? Rats?

MARA
Nothing.

MORT
How'd you like to die?

MARA
Wait!

> *Blurred focus: they are suspended between dream and waking.*

I need sleep.

MORT
Go to sleep.

MARA
I feel strange.

Again they mesh into the nightmare.

MORT
Hello, I'm your doctor. How do you feel?

MARA
My watch stopped.

MORT
That's messy. You need a big lead box.

MARA
I need a nap.

MORT
Nap. Ok. Procedures and risks involved. First we freeze you, make a small incision, insert a tube up the aorta, watch its progress by fluoroscope. Then we inject the dye. You'll feel a burning sensation for fifteen seconds. At this point you sometimes have a reaction, but it can't be proven until you die. Then we x-ray the remains, and before you clog we yank out the tubes and try to stop the blood. At this point you often think of tall buildings swaying in the wind. We try to keep you back from the edge, but there is a slight chance, say half of one percent, that you may lose your balance and fall.

MARA
Am I worried?

MORT
Twice a day.

MARA
Risk? Is there any risk?

MORT
There's always some risk. Less on a passbook account, but there you get only five and a half percent. Municipals are still a good buy, but if your inner city deteriorates, you're gonna have problems with flushing.

MARA
What about malignancy?

MORT
It's like inflation. Eats away at what you've got.

MARA
How long am I in for?

MORT
Well, you can put it in five-year certificates, but I'd recommend a shorter confinement unless you want long-term security at the cost of short-term inflammation.

MARA
Wait! We're not talking about money—

MORT
(grasping her hand voraciously) I am! I'm a doctor! How do you feel?

MARA
Confused!

MORT
(suddenly solicitous) That's natural. And I'd love to help you. I'd be more than willing to help you. But I'm a doctor. Medicine is not an exact science. Medicine is an art. I'm an artist.

MARA
It's cold.

MORT
You don't expect all painters to paint rosy pictures. You don't expect all writers to write happy endings.

MARA
Clammy.

MORT
There's comic medicine and there's serious medicine. My medicine makes a statement: NOBODY LIVES FOREVER!

MARA
Ahhhhhhh!

> He strangles her. She screams. They wake
> into reality, lying side by side in bed.

MORT
What's the matter?

MARA
I was dreaming. You were the doctor.

MORT
That's a laugh.

MARA
If you're the doctor you're safe. Nothing to lose.

MORT
Relax.

MARA
It's like auto mechanics. You never know.

MORT
Relax and get to sleep.

MARA
Beddy-bye.

MORT
And try not to yell when we start.

MARA
Start what?

MORT
Cutting.

> *Nightmare: he grabs her from behind, cuts her throat.*

MARA
Stop it! Stop! I'm the nurse!

MORT
(releasing her) Oh my God. Sorry. Here, let me button you up.

MARA
It's all right, I'm on the pill.

MORT
Thank God. Read me the appointments, we're behind schedule.

MARA
There's Mr. Pillsbury.

MORT

Mr. Pillsbury's cancer. I'm sick of his damn cancer.
Everybody's got a cancer. It's his funeral.

MARA

There's Mrs. Pillsbury, for an abortion.

MORT

How advanced is the pregnancy?

MARA

He'll be nineteen this fall.

MORT

Nurse, people have no respect for human life. They
don't deserve to live.

MARA

There's Dr. Pillsbury.

MORT

Dr. Pillsbury? That's not right. I'm Dr. Pillsbury.

MARA

You're on the list.

MORT

But I'm the doctor.

MARA

It's on the list.

MORT

You'll be sorry. I'm the doctor. I'll stand up and
shake your hand!

They clasp hands, shake violently.

BOTH

HELLO, I'M YOUR DOCTOR, HOW DO YOU FEEL?

Mort sinks down, Mara dominant.

MORT

Well. . . I don't feel any lumps. I really need to get
home. My driver's license expires on Friday, I have
to study for the test, I have to get my eyes opened.
Couldn't I still be the doctor?

MARA

I can't find the vein.

MORT
The grass needs mowing, it's getting too high to cut.

MARA
I can't find the vein.

MORT
It's growing too fast. The doctors are amazed.

MARA
I'm the doctor. I can't find the vein.

MORT
But Friday I'm due to expire!

MARA
Gotcha!

MORT
Ahhhhhhhhh!

They wake.

MARA
Bad dreams?

MORT
Doctors.

MARA
Relax.

Blurred focus.

MORT
I should have had it out. In school my friends had everything taken out. I should have done it then.

MARA
Are you the doctor or the patient?

MORT
I forgot.

MARA
It's safer to be the doctor.

MORT
Can he wear a white hat?

MARA
I'll be the doctor too. Then we're a team.

          MORT
A medical team.

          MARA
MD's!

          MORT
Men in white!

          MARA
Doctor!

          MORT
Doc!

          They embrace, then recoil.

          MARA
Oh dear, I contaminated you.

          MORT
I was sterile. Wait! The operation!

          Focusing on an imaginary patient:

But there's nobody here.

          MARA
That's ok. It's practice. Run scrimmage, get the
plays down pat, then we shove the patients under
there and let fly. We don't even check the face.

          MORT
Unless there's a beard. We don't want a beard in
the muck.

          MARA
What do you think? Rapid-Shave? Drano? E-Z-Off?

          MORT
Wait. He's not real. He's imaginary.

          MARA
Then we better work fast. You take the steak knife,
I've got the juicer.

          MORT
Roger!

          They begin burlesque surgery: broad, gross
          pantomime.

MARA
Take that out, I saw it move.

MORT
Arthritis. Out with his bones.

MARA
How about the kidneys?

MORT
Feel ok. Oh-oh, bed's wet. Can't have that.

MARA
You did a no-no.

MORT
Give'em the heave.

MARA
Squeeze that.

MORT
Not very fresh.

MARA
Mold.

MORT
Out.

MARA
Let's do a brain test. What are the three justifications for existence? Wrong. Take out the brain.

MORT
What about the liver?

MARA
We had liver last night.

MORT
Well, it's cheap.

MARA
Three dollars a pound?

MORT
For that we could buy sweetbreads.

MARA
He didn't complain of sweetbreads.

MORT
Out.

MARA
Better wash all this off.

MORT
Wait. I got a bite.

MARA
All we can do is pray.

MORT
Pull out the plug.

MARA
Locomotor ataxia.

MORT
Dynamite up the kazoo! Take cover!

Catastrophic explosion.

MARA
Got him.

MORT
Is he ok?

MARA
He's dead.

MORT
But he's imaginary.

MARA
He is now.

Blurred focus.

MORT
Hey, what am I doing? I'm not the doctor, I'm supposed to *see* the doctor. . .

MARA
No, come on, you better be the doctor. .

MORT
I can't speak Latin. I missed the test. Is there a
band-aid in the house?

MARA
We're running out of gas. . .

> *He transforms into a concrete character: a*
> *fatigued fiifty-year-old physician, speaking*
> *to us directly:*

MORT

I have a patient. Forty years old. Female. White.
The most radiant, life-loving woman I know.

MARA

She's a patient. She's dying.

MORT

She has leukemia. She's dying. I do bone-marrow
biopsies. Which are very painful. She's had remis-
sion twice. Then it goes on.

MARA

She's losing her looks.

MORT

She tries to joke.

MARA

Symptoms?

MORT

Symptoms? I feel a cold sweat. Shaking. I try to
laugh.

MARA

Prognosis?

MORT

Six months.

MARA

Side effects?

MORT

Side effects?

MARA

Any side effects?

MORT

You die.

MARA

Who dies?

MORT

The patient dies.

MARA
Who's the patient?

MORT
The patient pays the piper.

MARA
Then who pays the doctor?

MORT
Whoever's dying.

MARA
Everyone's dying.

> *Pause. Incredulous:*

MORT
No. . .

> *Stark awake, they kneel clumsily side by side on the bed, hands in prayer.*

I'm the patient now.

MARA
I'm the patient too.

> *They mumble in shambling unison:*

BOTH
YEA THOUGH I WALK THROUGH THE VALLEY OF
    THE SHADOW OF—
YEA THOUGH I WALK THROUGH THE VALLEY OF—
YEA THOUGH—
VALLEY OF—
SHA—
VA—
I FEAR NO EVIL!
NO EVIL.
YEA THOUGH I FEAR NO—
YEA THOUGH I FEAR NO—
YEA THOUGH I WALK THROUGH THE VALLEY OF
    THE SHADOW OF—

> *Their lips form a word, soundlessly. Fade.*

STUFF WE'RE SAVING UP

Two large galvanized metal garbage cans, with lids, center stage. Two actors enter as kids, playing.

CLIFF
Hey, you wanta have a club?

LIL
Ok.

CLIFF
Ok. We'll be the . . . Save-it-up Club. You have to save it up.

LIL
Save what?

CLIFF
Stuff you're saving up. Cause Mommy said, "Sure you have mean feelings. But those mean feelings are garbage, so you put those mean feelings in a garbage can, and you put the lid on tight."

They pick up the garbage cans, pretend.

LIL
And if we meet a monster, we open it up—

CLIFF
And it stinks the monster away.

LIL
I got all my mad stuff inside.

CLIFF
Go!

Rhythm. They march in place, faced front, keeping in step, carrying the garbage cans. At times they look off to the right, counting milestones.

BOTH
WE'RE THE SAVE-IT-UP CLUB, WE'RE THE SAVE-IT-UP CLUB. . .

> LIL

What's that?

> CLIFF

Five.

> LIL

No, six. I'm six.

> CLIFF

What's in yours?

> LIL

Mommy tried to make my hair curl, but it wouldn't curl, and she said it was my fault.

> CLIFF

My daddy won't buy me a Spiderman Racecar Set.

> LIL

My daddy spanked me for peppering the cat.

> CLIFF

That's a seven. Now I'm seven. Pretend it's heavy.

> LIL

It is.

> > *Abruptly, she gives up, sets the can down heavily.*

> CLIFF

You can't stop. This is the Save-it-up Club.

> LIL

So what?

> CLIFF

You have to save it up.

> > *After a moment, she lifts the garbage can again. They continue, still in step, but more shambling. The cans are heavier.*

> LIL

Did you get some new stuff?

> CLIFF

When they chose up sides, they chose me last.

> LIL

That's cause you're no good. They chose me first.

CLIFF
Yeh?

LIL
And I told my dad, and he said, "I guess that's supposed to be important." *(enraged)* I'm gonna dump this out!

CLIFF
No! We gotta save it up. Cause this is—

LIL
The Save-it-up Club. *(looking off)* What's that?

CLIFF
Ten. Happy birthday to me!

LIL
No, to me!

CLIFF
My teacher told me to put my head down on my desk and be ashamed for ten minutes.

LIL
My mom says I'm fat.

CLIFF
I do stuff with mine, like bopping. I bopped Denny McGurren.

LIL
Wow.

CLIFF
He was always bopping me, so I got mine real full and I bopped him, and he stayed bopped.

LIL
Christine's got a Ghostbusters one. It's the official one. I wanted that one, but I got Garfield instead.

CLIFF
Kevin's got a really neat one. It's not metal. It's genuine plastic.

LIL
(looking off) Fourteen.

CLIFF
(looking off) Fifteen.

Now they are teenagers. They walk in a
slow shuffle, out of step, becoming con-
scious of one another's closeness.

LIL

You wanta carry it for me?

CLIFF

Sure.

He takes each garbage can by a handle,
carries them on his back, nearly sinks un-
der the weight.

Wow!

LIL

I got a lot saved up. Hey, can you do the new—
Whatta they call it?

CLIFF

The Sludge. "Hey. Hey. Doin' the Sludge."

Both, in step, do a dumpy, slouching side-
step back and forth, continuing.

LIL

Everybody's doing that one. All the neat kids.

CLIFF

Hey, remember . . . the Save-it-up Club?

LIL

No. Yeh. "You gotta save it up." That was dumb.

Exhausted, he returns her garbage can.
They resume their walk.

CLIFF

Hey, did you see that creepy, what's his name. . .
Conroy?

LIL

Yuck.

CLIFF

He doesn't keep the lid on. He just carries it around
in his hands.

LIL

Dorrie called him, and pretended to be Cynthia, and
asked him to a party, and he fell for it, and went to

Cynthia's, and she was there with Ted! He carried
that for a week, where everybody could smell it.

CLIFF
What's that? *(looking off)* Seventeen.

LIL
Eighteen.

CLIFF
Nineteen.

LIL
Oh-oh.

CLIFF
Huh?

LIL
I think we went too far.

CLIFF
Oh.

> *They halt, then join hands over the cans,
> walk solemnly in a wedding march.*

LIL
It is a burden.

CLIFF
Yes it is.

LIL
But I think we're ready to accept.

CLIFF
To accept, believe, and share.

> *They stop, face one another.*

LIL
I will take your bad vibes to be my bad vibes.

CLIFF
And yours to be mine.

> *They kiss each other's garbage cans. The
> cans suddenly become very heavy. They
> walk in flat-footed unison.*

I've never been so happy.

LIL
I'm speechless.

CLIFF
Sure, commitment is a burden, but if we share—

LIL
Excuse me, honey—

CLIFF
We'll grow as people.

LIL
I think I'm having some babies—

CLIFF
(more and more energetic) Starting to find myself.

LIL
(more and more drained) Honey, I'm—

CLIFF
Really sailing along!

LIL
I feel so—

CLIFF
Full of this creative energy!

LIL
I can't stand it—

CLIFF
But you do a terrific job!

LIL
It's so heavy—

CLIFF
But you go right along, because a woman's center of
gravity is lower than a man's. You're lower than me
so you don't have as high to lift.

LIL
(looking off) Twenty-nine.

CLIFF
(looking off) Thirty.

   Silence. They stop.

LIL
Isn't that cute? Billy's got a wastebasket. Jenny's got a coffee can.

CLIFF
With a lid.

> *They continue walking. Occasionally one misses a beat, then manages to stumble back into step.*

Sleepy?

LIL
I want to stop.

CLIFF
Huh?

LIL
We've been so stupid. Trudging along with this horrible, repulsive, stinking dead weight. Why can't we just dump it? Haul it away.

CLIFF
We'd need a professional.

LIL
I don't care. I want to begin to live.

CLIFF
Shoes.

LIL
Huh?

CLIFF
It's your shoes. You need new shoes. Shoes that breathe.

LIL
No, I need—

CLIFF
Good basic arch supports. Honey, you're hefting a lotta weight there. You've got major responsibilities. You need arch supports.

LIL
Heavy duty. Maybe heavy duty arch supports.

                CLIFF
With suction soles, all those little suckers that grab
and grip and clutch on, and shoe liners, sheep's
wool, fiberglas. Then you'd be warm, you'd be dry,
and you'd be about five inches taller.

                LIL
I'll give it a try. . .

                CLIFF
You can do it.

                    *She starts to walk with a spring. He jogs to
                    catch up, becoming more exhausted as she
                    sails and glides, elated.*

                LIL
It's so . . . liberating!

                CLIFF
Rejuvenating.

                LIL
Resurrecting!

                CLIFF
Thirty-five.

                LIL
Thirty-six.

                CLIFF
Thirty-seven.

                LIL
Thirty-eight.

                CLIFF
Etcetera.

                    *Dead halt. Pause. They adjust their grip
                    on the cans to minimize back strain, take a
                    deep breath, then continue, heavily.*

That's a new one.

                LIL
I went shopping.

                CLIFF
What'd it cost?

LIL

Well I feel it's a necessity. I could go on with that old battered thing, but I have nothing to wear that matches it, and look, this is indoor-outdoor.

CLIFF

Thirty gallons. That's a lot.

LIL

It's not that much. You know, around Christmas, all the unpleasantness, things pile up. The plastic ones aren't nearly so nice.

CLIFF

Plastic ones have an advantage though. They're modern.

LIL

Some people are naming theirs.

CLIFF

Billy didn't call.

LIL

Jenny called. We had a fight. She's dating a boy with a dumpster.

Cans suddenly become very, very heavy.
They plod. He mutters under his breath.
She tries to ignore it, but can't.

Are you upset?

CLIFF

I'm not upset. I'm just a little . . . upset.

LIL

This will last as long as we do.

CLIFF

But what's it doing to us? We thought it's just a game. We thought sure, once the kids are grown we can sort it out. But the attic, there's forty-two cans up there!

LIL

We'll take a weekend.

CLIFF

We keep saying that.

LIL
All right, then chuck it! I wanted to long ago. From
now on, when you've got something, just lay it out!

CLIFF
Right on the table!

LIL
Stink and all!

CLIFF
Plain sight!

LIL
Clear it up!

CLIFF
Face it!

> *They stop, think. After a long think, they*
> *continue plodding, exactly as before.*

Is that a manual or an automatic?

LIL
Well, you hold it so it's manual. But it gets to be
automatic.

CLIFF
I need a new one.

LIL
You could buy it on time.

CLIFF
I don't have much time.

> *In simultaneous collapse, they drop cans to*
> *the floor. Immensely relieved, they rest a*
> *moment Then they position themselves, be-*
> *gin to push the cans forward, as if pushing*
> *a dead vehicle, though still in place.*

LIL
That's much better.

CLIFF
Second wind.

LIL
(looking off) Fifty-two.

CLIFF
Can't be fifty-two.

LIL
(squinting) Sixty-two.

CLIFF
No.

LIL
Save-it-up Club.

CLIFF
What?

LIL
It was so cute. I was taking care of the babies for
Jennie, and they made up a club, called the Save-it-
up Club. To be in the Save-it-up Club you have to
save it all up.

CLIFF
Save what?

LIL
All kinds of nonsense.

> *They fall to their knees. Hobbling on their
> knees, they continue pushing at the cans.
> They are very old.*

CLIFF
Can you see the marker?

LIL
I left my glasses.

CLIFF
I see it.

LIL
What does it say?

CLIFF
It's got my name on it.

LIL
Oh dear. And mine?

CLIFF
I can't tell. If I could just . . . stop shoving this . . .
damn garbage can!

LIL

It's your legacy.

CLIFF

Legacy?

LIL

Legacy. You've carried it all your life. It stank, but you went right on. You filled it, you kept filling it, you never let off the lid. So what earthly right do your children have, or your children's children and theirs, to come along and get off easy? You carried it, they can carry it. You did it, they'll do it. It's your legacy, and they'll pass it on, with interest.

CLIFF

I wish. . .

LIL

I know. . .

CLIFF

I always. . .

LIL

Never the time. . .

CLIFF

Nor the guts. . .

LIL

I might. . .

CLIFF

Too late.

LIL

Never.

CLIFF

Together?

LIL

Together?

CLIFF

Why not?

> Dead halt. They open the lids of the cans,
> reach in, take out plastic toy machine guns.
> They machine-gun the audience.

BOTH
ACKATA ACKATA ACKATA ACKATA ACKATA ACKA-
TA ACKATA ACKATA ACKATA ACKATA ACKATA
BUDA BUDA BUDA BUDA BUDA BUDA BUDA BUDA
BUDA BUDA BUDA BUDA BUDA BUDA BUDA BUDA
BUDA AAAAAAAAAAAAAAAAAAAAA!

Nothing happens. They squint.

LIL
What do you think?

CLIFF
It misses the mark.

LIL
You think we'll be in the news?

CLIFF
It's not news any more.

LIL
Oh dear. I did so want a happy ending.

> *Silence. They raise the empty cans, put*
> *them over their heads, stand, appearing to*
> *be garbage cans with legs.*
>
> *Blackout.*

A USER'S GUIDE

This appendix aims, hopelessly, at imparting the accumulated wisdom of twenty years of performing. But the only real message is *Just Do It*. Reading this won't make the cake rise; that comes from seeking these human hearts. But, for what it's worth. . .

Routining

How do you put these acts together to make a full show? That question preceded every performance we've done for the last twenty years. It depends on the length, the expected audience, the location, and above all, what you really have a burning lust to say.

It's possible to structure a show with broad entertainment appeal that still leads the audience into more challenging territory. This requires careful "routining," a sense of how the audience, at the end of each piece, catches the trapeze bar to swing to the next. Or it's possible to present the acts as separate entities, weighted toward the bizarre. However, we would warn against a full evening of the weightiest pieces only. Even a hip audience needs a breather sometimes.

It may be helpful to sketch the back-and-forth of structuring a hypothetical show. Let's assume it's a full-evening show, with a fairly small cast, for an adult audience accustomed to conventional theatre; they're expecting to be entertained, albeit in an offbeat way.

For Openers. . .

Dreamers or **Questions** give a broad thematic fanfare to the show, and a direct address mode that rivets focus. The first is shorter, the second is better if we want to introduce the whole ensemble.

But would this audience be more comfortable with a conventional sketch to start with? **Entrepreneur** is good, or **Dalmatian**, though the latter is long for an opener — better a structure with simpler development. **Bon Voyage** might predispose the audience, through its use of stereotypes, to expect a different sort of show.

This time, we opt for **Dreamers**, giving a simple, direct view of the personal roots of the acts.

For Closers:

What's our final destination? Many possibilities, though few upbeat pieces with a sense of finality —

Peace Negotiations might work. The kaleidoscopic **Questions** doesn't end cheerfully, but it does bring the whole ensemble into a summary statement.

A show doesn't require an "upbeat" finish to give the audience a sense of energy. It has to do more with strength and completion. **Shadow** or **Stuff** have strong rhythmic finality, whereas **Miss Bleep** would end the show on a discord. **Monopoly** or **Factory Dance** have weight, but the former has a nasty after-taste, and the latter is very dependent on its acting: it can be moving or it can just be brutal.

We decide to end on **Questions**, with a weightier "star act" before it. Candidates are **Factory Dance** and **Monopoly** — both exhausting emotionally. But will the actors have the energy to play the final piece, and will the audience agree to be battered? **Doors** or **Stuff** are proposed as options. At last it comes down to the question: which do we really *want* to do?

Back-Tracking:

Our next linchpins are the acts directly before and after intermission. **Peace Negotiations** might end Act One: intermission at this locale is for socializing, and we don't want to cast a pall over the lobby.

To begin Act Two, we decide on a straight situation sketch, comic in tone, to ease them back into the show, perhaps **Dalmatian**, **Tell It** or **Entrepreneur**. But maybe not. If we aim for a more emotionally intense Act Two, we might better jack up the energy with **Miss Bleep** or **Doom** — funny but surreal.

Filling in the slots? With an opening litany such as **Dreamers**, the next act wants to have a situation the audience grasps easily. **Condemned** might work as the second piece in Act Two, but not in the same slot in Act One — *unless* to prepare us for an unusual show texture, in which case it might be just right.

Some acts are serious but with a very human feel; others are abrasive and push us away. Same for comedy: **Entrepreneur** is warm and amiable, **Watchers** distanced. The producer must consider the emotional *intimacy* of the material when arranging a show, not just the balance between comic and serious.

Bridges

A show of short acts is appealing to audiences, but also taxing, because they are jolted continually into new worlds, digest an effect while preparing to jump to the next, like a one-week European vacation. Unlike some revues, there's no fluff filler, so we can rarely consume more than eight acts in one evening without bloating, and that's pushing it.

The producer needs to plan what happens *between* sketches. At the simplest, we performed FAMILIES with no light changes, no bridges: at the end of an act, we froze a moment, turned front to acknowledge (and signal) applause, then reset in full light, took positions and started the new act. Probably the only absolute is not to leave the audience without some sort of undemanding visual focus as they digest. Other devices:

* *Blackouts, followed by bridge music* as actors, in dim light, reset furniture, giving the audience time to assimilate the last piece. Since the show's "story" is an ensemble telling a number of stories about life, it's appropriate to see them *preparing* to tell those stories.

* *Bridges comprised of short litanies* (in the manner of **Dreamers**, culled from newspapers, road signs, etc. This works if the "found" material is well selected and is more "background music" than a new unit — otherwise it becomes a new act requiring engaged attention, and its function is lost.

* *Spoken introductions.* There's nothing wrong with talking to the audience. We've used anecdotes to link acts with personal realities, even to state, baldly, the intended theme: "The next sketch is about that moment when we shut a door that stays shut for years." But it's important that the phrasing has a hook. Avoid blandness — "This is about problems old people face in living with their kids" — that lies like leftover pasta. They won't laugh much after a minute of silent prayer.

Setting & Lights

Every act in this collection has been performed, some time or another, in locales offering *no* set and *no* lighting except for visibility. And they've worked. So the bare minimum is a platform, a passion, and a couple of folding chairs.

While we've had actors simply sitting at the edge of the playing area, rising at cue, it's preferable to have curtains or backdrops for entrances and exits. But the simpler the better. Real walls or decorative dressings tend to emphasize the separation of sketch from sketch rather than their unity of purpose.

Large stages can be intimidating when presenting intimate work, but we've played on them many times. The director shouldn't try to "fill" the stage but rather to give the action its natural dynamic. Even two people sitting at a desk can create a small, intense, bright energy in the middle of cavernous space; our visual scope will shrink to that proportion, as it does when we watch TV. The action should be brought forward as far as possible; if there's poor lighting on the stage apron, the director should consider footlights. These are out of fashion in realistic tradition, but they're perfectly appropriate to this work.

There's advantage to be gained from a sense that actors are out there, unarmed, with nothing but stories they want to tell. Designers sometimes go for glitzy colors, thinking "revues" are all alike, or for ingenious shifting panels. But the simpler the better. We've used sets created from a dozen doors, from clothing on hangers, from cut-out silhouettes, from blow-ups of news clippings — metaphors of human debris.

Interpretation

As mentioned, these acts sketch choices in human behavior; they're not vehicles to show an actor's range of emotional expression. Of course the characters have an inner life, but very self-contradictory. The principal in **Dalmatian** sympathizes with the student, yet is overwhelmed by rage, then despair at having bungled so badly. Her feelings are intensified, not lessened, by the fact that they contradict her intentions.

Likewise, the audience is split in its own response. One moment the principal is victimizer, the next a victim. One director wanted to cut the principal's phone talk with her child, feeling that it wasn't funny — missing the point, of course, that the speech is there to *humanize* her, not to caricature. That same distortion can happen without line cuts: an actress once gave the "ten-thirty bell" speech a very pompous tone, ignoring the irony that the woman fully understands her own absurdity, but feels helpless to avoid it.

Casting

This chart indicates the most common casting in our performances; these are recommended. The noted options require minor line changes. A single revue can include anywhere from two actors to a dozen or more.

	M	F	Variants
Peace Negotiations		2	
Miss Bleep	*2	*2	Students M or F
Tell It Like It Is	1	1	
Dalmatian		*2	Either role M or F
Factory Dance	*1	*2	Varying # of workers
Anniversary	1	1	
Bon Voyage	1	2	
Watchers	1	2	
Doors	1	1	
Dreamers	1	1	
Entrepreneur	1	1	
Nina, Ray & Earl	2	1	
Monopoly	2	2	
Condemned	*1	*1	M.C. could be F
Questions	*2	*2	Varying # of actors
Doom	*2	*1	Duo could be M or F
Shadow	1	1	
Stuff We're Saving	1	1	

Text Changes

Copyright forbids changes without the authors' consent. But we ourselves have often made cuts for particular circumstances. We don't object to very minor cuts or alterations required by atypical casting or allergy to four-letter words: there are times when the whole sense of a piece is lost while the audience worries, "Did they just say *that*?" Use your best judgment. But cutting for *time* is dangerous. The acts are honed to the bone. We've condensed them at times, especially for radio, but it's better simply to do fewer pieces.

One way to solve problems is to ask the authors. As long as we can call collect, we're happy to answer questions. One teacher gathered courage to call, asking us to explain a line she thought was intended as funny but passed her by. That's the professional way to do it; we were happy that someone in Ohio had the dedication to get that line right. Gifted directors often ask simple-minded questions — that's part of being gifted. It's useful to know how others wrangle with our work, so while Ibsen can't return your calls, we will.

Conrad Bishop & Elizabeth Fuller, after five years of college teaching, were co-founders of Milwaukee's Theatre X and in 1974 formed The Independent Eye, which they continue to direct. Bishop's play **Wanna** was showcased at the 1980 O'Neill National Playwrights Conference, and **Dreambelly** was produced in 1981 by Theatre X and toured The Netherlands under auspices of Amsterdam's Mickery Theatre. His audiovisual work, in association with Elizabeth Fuller — also a theatre composer with 25 scores to her credit — has received production awards from the Corporation for Public Broadcasting, American Personnel & Guidance Association, and American Bar Association, and **Families** was recipient of a 1982 Ohio State Award, a top international broadcast honor. Their radio series **The Want Ads** has been broadcast by public stations nationwide. In 1982, **Full Hookup** was the co-winner of Actors Theatre of Louisville's Great American Play Contest and was presented in ATL's Festival of New American Plays, directed by Jon Jory, and at New York's Circle Repertory under the direction of Marshall Mason. **Smitty's News**, directed by Bishop, was presented at the 1986 Humana Festival. Their plays have also been presented by Fulton Opera House, Walnut Street Theatre, Denver Center Theatre, Florida Studio Theatre, American Theatre Arts, New Arts Theatre of Dallas, and others. They have received four fellowships from Pennsylvania Council on the Arts and were 1985 recipients of a National Endowment for the Arts Playwriting Fellowship.

Theatre X, a Milwaukee ensemble founded in 1969, is one of America's oldest and most respected experimental theatres, receiving an Obie Award for **A Fierce Longing**. It has presented 40 major productions and 100 shorter works, including eleven world premieres at the renowned Mickery Theatre in Amsterdam; has collaborated with Stockholm's Jordcirkus; and has toured England, Wales, and The Netherlands, as well as 24 states of the U.S.

The Independent Eye is a Lancaster theatre and media arts center. Since 1974, the Eye has performed in 33 states, has appeared at New York's CSC, Chicago's Body Politic, Baltimore Theatre Project, Philadelphia's Painted Bride and Movement Theatre International, and as focus for social issues projects from Flagstaff to Jerusalem. In 1977, the Eye moved from Chicago to Lancaster, opening the Eye Theatre Works in 1982. The Eye was one of ten theatres in the U.S. selected for the 1985 National Endowment for the Arts Advancement Program.